T0154157

the secret life

A BOOK OF WISDOM FROM THE GREAT TEACHER

the secret life

JEFFREY KATZ

WITH ALYS YABLON WYLEN

Humanix Books

The Secret Life

ISBN: 978-1-63006-136-4 (Hard Cover)
ISBN: 978-1-63006-107-4 (Trade Paper)
ISBN: 978-1-63006-108-1 (E-book)

Printed in the United States of America

10 9 8 7 6 5 4 3 2 1

To my mother, who gave me the key,

and to my father, who showed me what to open

CONTENTS

CONTENTS

INTRODUCTION

MAIMONIDES AND THE SECRET LIFE

At times the truth shines so brilliantly that we perceive it as clear as day. Our nature and habit then draw a veil over our perception, and we return to a darkness almost as dense as before. We are like those who, though beholding frequent flashes of lightning, still find themselves in the thickest darkness of the night.

MAIMONIDES

TWO MEN AWAIT their train on the subway platform in New York City. They are dressed in business suits. Each holds a newspaper folded under one arm, and both are staring at their cell phones. To the casual observer, one might think that these two men lead similar lives. Jobs on Wall Street, perhaps. Apartments on the Upper East Side, complete with wives and children and gym memberships. Let's assume for a moment that they do in fact share those basic circumstances, with the same jobs and the same salaries.

The first man—let's call him Joe—is heading home a little earlier than usual at the end of a long week at work. Just like every other day this week, Joe is spending his commuting time checking his stock profile on his smartphone. Obsessed with the fluctuations in the market, Joe is constantly refreshing his feed, counting his pennies, and planning his next move. Joe has always had a comfortable life, and he plans to maintain his wealth forever. In fact, it is his main goal in life to earn ever more money so that he can buy a bigger apartment for his family, own the newest gadgets, and take the most lavish vacations.

Joe's wife has sent him three text messages so far this afternoon: one a picture of their son hanging upside down on the monkey bars, one a voice recording from their daughter about her science fair project, and one a reminder that they are going to a fund-raising gala tonight, and the babysitter is arriving in 10 minutes. He hasn't read, or even noticed, any of the messages yet.

Meanwhile, the other man, Ted, is exchanging text messages with his wife, Nancy. He is on his way to the soup kitchen, where he volunteers to serve dinner to the homeless once a week, and he tells Nancy that he will pick up ice cream on his way home for movie night with the kids. He wants to know what flavor they like best this week, and which movie is at the top of their wish list. Ever since he spent a harrowing week living in his car years ago, Ted has vowed to give as much time and money as possible to the place where he was able to get a warm meal on those seven long, cold nights. Now a successful banker with a fine home and a loving family, Ted has stayed true to his word and not only writes generous checks to the soup kitchen but also rolls up his sleeves week after week to work there.

Ted appreciates his good fortune and knows that poverty is never as far away as you might think. Because he has experienced significant hardship, he does not take his lifestyle for granted, and he makes sure to save money for his children and wife in case of emergency. He also knows that giving money to those in need, even in small amounts, not only helps the recipients of that money, but also does good for his soul. Giving of his time and energy is just as rewarding, and he plans to instill these values in his own children as they mature.

The two men, though outwardly similar, have vastly different approaches to life. On the subjects of wealth, family, and dedication to a higher purpose, they could not be further apart. Joe works hard to ensure that he is as wealthy as possible, even if it means long stretches away from his wife and kids. He gives money to charity, attending glamorous events that cost thousands of dollars to plan and are as much about socializing and glitz as they are about raising money for worthy causes. When he votes, he makes sure to endorse the candidates who promise tax cuts for the wealthy, without much thought to other issues. Joe has never had to struggle, and he has not made an effort to empathize with those who do.

Ted recalls his own experience of near-homelessness and financial hardship and prioritizes meaningful volunteer work and pointed charity as a result, while making sure to appreciate his wife and children and to schedule special family time together. He lobbies local government officials to fight for employment opportunities, fair wages, and affordable housing for his city. He tries to live his life with a sense of gratitude and feels a strong desire to contribute to his community.

Which man has a greater sense of accomplishment and self-worth at the end of the day? If you had a choice between the two lifestyles, which would you choose? When we think about how to make our lives more meaningful, and how to make a difference in the world around us, we are quickly overwhelmed by all the options before us and all the competing priorities we hold.

It might seem easy to point to Ted as the more admirable of the two men, and to say that given the choice, we would be generous with our wealth and humble in our actions. But for the vast majority of us, if we are being honest, our natural instincts are actually closer to Joe's. In our quest for survival, we are drawn to "more" rather than "less." With even the best of intentions, it is difficult to part with our hard-earned money, and perhaps even harder to spare what little free time today's frenetic world leaves for us.

In this book, we will discover how to access a deep sense of fulfillment by doing good for yourself and the world around you through the humblest of acts and the quietest of thoughts. There is a world of unseen benefits in giving of yourself, loving others, seeking justice, discovering and then working toward your own higher calling. All these acts lead to achieving a developed level of resilience. By following this path, you can literally change your life and the lives of those around you forever. As with Joe and Ted, different approaches to life can impact your particular personality and the development of your inner character. The choices we make every day, and the actions we take, have far-reaching consequences, even though only a fraction of those consequences are immediately apparent.

The Outer World and the Secret Life

The world we live in is relentless. Every day is filled with instantaneous access to information, endless streams of consciousness vying for our attention. Our inner lives are often as tumultuous and overloaded as our daily schedules, and we are compelled to broadcast our every move for all to see.

The pressure that this kind of existence puts upon us can feel overwhelming and stressful even on good days. Not only do we expect ourselves to balance more than ever before—careers, families, fitness goals, and political engagement, to name a few of our preoccupations—we live in an age when social media allows others to observe and critique everything we do, say, or think, so that our lives become a sort of unintended public performance.

Gone, it seems, are the days of privacy and quiet reflection. In this world of constant contact, we have never been more isolated and lonely, and a plague of depression and anxiety is sweeping over us. This can feel overwhelming and upsetting, and also impossible to remedy as our society continues to evolve and speed up day after day.

The good news is that it doesn't have to be this way. There is another life simmering just below the surface of this existence. This life, the Secret Life, has been available to us all along, but we have pushed it aside in our rush to check things off our to-do lists. It is a life in which we strive to discover and develop our most noble selves, to define our sense of justice and infuse our lives with higher purpose, all while intention-ally *not* publishing online updates on every goal we reach.

Learning to keep the right things a secret will bring about the most dramatic benefits you can imagine. We tend to keep our negative experiences private and to broadcast only positive things for all the world to see. As a result, we publicly tout our "best" selves at all times, and this can lead to jealousy, competition, and worse.

If we are honest, our experiences are never as simplified and rosy as they may seem to be on our Facebook profile. One mother I know joked, "If only I could admit that behind the camera that took a photo of my adorable toddler eating a beautiful homemade cookie, there were piles of unwashed dishes, a crying baby sitting in a dirty diaper, and toys strewn about on every surface." We don't publicize the messes in our lives or the confusion in our hearts. We keep all of that, all of the hurt and the disappointment and the self-doubt, to ourselves. And those are the thoughts that keep us up at night and damage our souls the most.

But what if, instead, we flipped things around? What if we kept the good things we did, like the perfect chocolate chip cookies we bake, private, and instead publicized the messy reality of the rest of our day?

I believe that shifting the focus of our inner lives from negative to positive can be life-altering and ultimately world-changing. Knowing inside, even if no one else will ever know, that you helped a struggling child go home with nutritious food to eat and books to read over the weekend, will warm your soul and give you the confidence and belief in yourself that you may otherwise lack. The beauty of the Secret Life is that it can slowly but surely shift your perceptions about yourself and reveal yourself at your best.

By embracing the idea of a Secret Life, a litany of acts and attitudes that are deeply felt but kept private, we can give ourselves the gifts of true self-confidence and resilience, two of the most sought-after and rewarding characteristics around.

An Ancient Wisdom for Our Days

Only one figure since the time of the Bible has ever been honored and celebrated by all three major Western religions. That person is Maimonides.

A philosopher, rabbi, physician, religious thinker, and logician who had mastered all the best science of his day, Maimonides was a "Renaissance man" centuries before the Renaissance. He believed deeply in the dignity and potential of all people. All noble individuals of any nation, he insisted, have the same high worth and sacred standing in the eyes of God. The achievements of noble people, those who serve as models and teachers of virtue, kindness, and truth, depend on their pursuit of individual nobility, the desire to live rich lives based on core beliefs and principles, and not on the nation, race, or ethnic group from which they arise.

Born in 1135 in Cordoba, Spain, Moses ben Maimon (later known as the Rambam, or Maimonides) fled his home as a child to avoid persecution. His family wandered for many years through western Africa and Morocco and finally settled in Egypt. His first major work, a commentary on the Oral Torah, was composed while on this journey, often while his family was experiencing profound poverty and homelessness. His next publication, a controversial 14-volume legal code that organized the vast complex of Jewish biblical and rabbinic law in such a way as to make it accessible to those without elaborate academic backgrounds, was completed by the time he was 45 years old and was written while he studied medicine and rose to become so well respected as a doctor that he served as the court physician to the sultan Saladin.

As if those accomplishments weren't enough, the publication of his third and final masterpiece, *The Guide for the Perplexed*, was the culmination of Maimonides' life's work, and it would leave its mark on humanity for generations to come. St. Thomas Aquinas and other influential religious leaders were deeply affected by the work and philosophy of Maimonides. By the time he died at the age of 69 in 1204, he had achieved a towering stature among thinkers from all walks of life. Expressing the notion that he was the greatest sage to have lived since Moses of the Bible, his tomb in Israel is inscribed with the words, "From Moses to Moses there arose none like Moses."

Despite having lived over 800 years ago, Maimonides comes across as a distinctly modern thinker. He was the first religious authority to understand many biblical stories as allegories rather than literal truth, a notion so controversial in medieval times that he was labeled a heretic and his books were even burned. His understanding that all of us in this life, regardless of religion, country of origin, or social stature, are part of the tapestry of a larger universe, all working toward a common cause, was radical and groundbreaking. He taught that all human beings are capable of hearing the internal call to rise and act according to their noblest nature. Those individuals who live life as their best selves redeem, as it were, all of humanity. Humanity is, in this sense, an organic whole, much as the universe and world themselves are. Everything is interdependent.

Two characteristic teachings in *The Guide for the Perplexed* were to love God unconditionally and to do noble deeds and good works without any thought of reward. Maimonides taught that ample rewards, both material and spiritual, would indeed come, but that these must not motivate or affect the quality of one's behavior. His main concern was helping fellow thinkers discover their best selves, achieve their most noble accomplishments, and in turn change the world for the better, all while living a humble and peaceful life. These are pursuits that we still prioritize hundreds of years later, and yet it can seem like we are further than ever from accomplishing those lofty goals.

This book will illuminate the ancient teachings of Maimonides as they apply to our contemporary lives. We will see how making conscious choices to change our actions can lead to shifts in our mindset, and soon enough to societal changes for the better. The secret here is just that: keeping things secret. Life-altering change cannot come about by advertising accomplishments in mass media outlets. Rather, doing things for the grander purpose of improving the world works best when we cultivate a quiet, internal awareness of our choices and actions, rather than an external proclamation.

The Five Secrets

This book is divided into five chapters, one on each of the five secrets that can change your life and, by extension, the world in which we live. Each of these five subjects—*charity*, *justice*, *unconditional love*, *higher calling*, and *resilience*—is a core concept in the teachings of Maimonides. Discussed and debated since ancient times, these subjects are as relevant and interesting today as ever before.

In each chapter, you will learn how to change the way you think about and act upon your personal beliefs and values in these areas, and how such actions can lead to profound shifts in personal as well as global consciousness.

The benefits of living the Secret Life are countless. Changing your approaches to giving charity, to seeking justice, to loving others, and to believing in yourself enough to find and act on your higher calling will lead you to reach a level of resilience that will keep you grounded when you face difficulties and challenges. This is, quite literally, life-changing.

Best of all, it is never too late to start. Maimonides taught that as one ages, one's intellect becomes stronger and purer, and one's joy from that knowledge increases. With the added benefit of time and life experience, older adults are perhaps the most ideal practitioners of the Secret Life. Even if you feel that you have lived the majority of your life in a certain pattern that repeats itself time and again, the older you grow, the more intimately you know yourself and what matters most to you, and the more prepared you will be to accomplish great things.

So many success stories have begun later in life: Laura Ingalls Wilder published the first book in her Little House series at the age of 65, Julia Child learned to cook at age 40 and didn't become a television host until she was 50, and Stan Lee, creator of Spider-Man and other Marvel superheroes, wrote his first comic books in his 40s, and to this day—at the age of 95—he enjoys a cameo appearance in every major motion film made about one of his characters. Even Moses, that great biblical figure to whom Maimonides was compared on his tombstone, wasn't called by God to lead the Jewish people until he was 80 years old!

This goes to show that no matter when you start to practice the principles of the Secret Life, you can achieve great success. Whether you are 20 or 60, if you are willing to work on making better decisions, balancing your priorities, and dedicating yourself to a meaningful cause, you will see substantial change and success. Of course, we can never know how long we have in this life. But we should strive to never fall prey to the mentality that "time is running out, so why bother?" Humans now live longer and more productively than ever before. Age, as they say, is nothing but a number. And the greater your number, the greater your chances of making significant improvements in the world.

Are you ready to accomplish great things and change your whole outlook on life? If so, I urge you to quiet your mind, clear your desk, and spend some time evaluating how you have been approaching things until now, and how you can adjust your actions and choices to reflect a more ideal state. What you will find may just be the greatest secret of all.

CHAPTER ONE

THE SECRET OF CHARITY

Give a man a fish and he will eat for one day.

Teach a man to fish, and you feed him for a lifetime.

ATTRIBUTED TO MAIMONIDES

THE SECRET OF CHARITY

WHEN WE THINK about giving charity, the images that come to mind are often simple and straightforward: dropping coins into a red iron kettle on a winter day while a bell sounds in the background, phoning in a donation that qualifies for the gift of a tote bag, or buying an extra can of tuna fish or jar of peanut butter at the grocery store during a food drive. In other words, we more often think of "giving a man a fish," or helping someone solve an immediate problem, than "teaching a man to fish," or changing someone's long-term reality for the better. The idea that helping a person develop the skills and experience that will lead to employment and self-reliance is ideal is not a new one. In fact, this wisdom has been adopted by numerous cultures throughout the world for centuries.

The old adage, quoted above, "Give a man a fish and he will eat for one day. Teach a man to fish, and you feed him for a lifetime" is universally appealing. While the source of this wisdom is ultimately unknown, it has been attributed to Chinese, Italian, and Native American traditions and to such famous thinkers as Lao-Tzu and Maimonides. Wherever it comes from, what it teaches us is a major component of what I call the Secret of Charity.

The Eight Levels of Charity

Maimonides discussed charity at length, describing it as the ultimate sign of a righteous person and one of the most important acts of humanity. Assuming that everyone is obligated to give charity according to his or her means, and that we are also obligated to do everything in our power to avoid being in need ourselves, he described Eight Levels of Giving to help us develop our charitable tendencies. At the lowest levels, the giver spends less than what he or she can reasonably afford and does so begrudgingly. In these situations, both the giver and the recipient see each other, and there is no attempt at anonymity. In every subsequent level, the attitude of the giver becomes more genuine, and the distance between specific donors and recipients becomes greater, so that one is not burdened with pride, and the other is free of the guilt or shame that might accompany recognition.

The highest, most ideal level of giving is the one in which your charity enables someone to ultimately become self-supporting. Teaching a person to "fish"—giving someone the knowledge he or she needs to hold a job and function in society—is the greatest kindness one person can bestow on another. As Maimonides taught, we can "anticipate charity by preventing poverty."

Imagine what might happen to you if you were truly struggling financially. In times of uncertainty, we often find our thoughts quickly spiraling from one seemingly small problem to huge, overarching crises. While staring at a notice about a late car payment, you may begin to worry about the chain of events that might soon unfold. If you are unable to make your car payment, you might just lose the car. If you lose your car, how will you get to work? If you can't get to work, you will lose your job. If you lose your job, you might not be able to pay your rent. And so forth. Before long, you are worried about everything, and you begin to panic. In that moment, you don't just want a way to pay one month's worth of a car loan. You want a way to shore up your whole situation. Ideally, you want to render the worst-case scenario impossible to begin with.

When we put ourselves in the position to help others, the best thing we can do is to anticipate the "worst-case scenario" and try to prevent it from coming to fruition. While giving people the means to help solve their immediate problems is always appreciated, helping them get to a state in which they no longer face those problems is even better. When we try to stand in the shoes of someone who is struggling, forward-looking and preventative help is what we would want most for ourselves.

One person who has certainly reached the highest levels of charitable giving is Oprah Winfrey, the billionaire who started out a poor girl in the rural South, a victim of emotional and physical abuse. She worked her way up to become one of the most successful and well-loved people in recent history. Oprah is famous for her generosity. She has donated literally millions of dollars to a variety of worthy causes. Of the many amazing acts of giving she has performed, perhaps the most admirable are the schools she has established and funded for underprivileged children in African communities where none previously existed. She has helped countless girls reach their life goals by providing merit-based scholarships—grants given to students who have proved their academic prowess alongside their financial need.

Oprah's scholarships are not just tangible gifts. They recognize the hard work and effort of the recipients and help to ease the burdens of young women who would otherwise have to work several jobs while trying to focus on their studies. With the strain of paying for school lifted, recipients of Oprah's scholarships can direct more of their energy to learning and developing their chosen professions. Rather than just feeding them fish for a day, Oprah has enabled these children to find their own fish, a gift that will last a lifetime. These students have been given the gift of education, and with it the chance to improve their lives and the lives of those in their family and community.

The Anonymous Gift

When British singer and songwriter George Michael died unexpectedly in 2016 at the age of 53, his fans and fellow musicians were stunned. A star since his early days in the band Wham!, Michael was often the subject of tabloid sensationalism, and stories about his private life were published mercilessly for all to see. Despite these damaging stories in the press, however, Michael created groundbreaking music and garnered enormous fame and fortune. But in the days following his untimely death, another kind of story began to flood the Internet about George Michael, this time about a side of him that had never been featured in any of those glitzy magazines.

George Michael, it seemed, had been giving away millions of pounds every year in secret donations, all with the express direction that he not be given credit for doing so. Stories poured out on Twitter from people like the barmaid who was left a tip of £5,000 after she had mentioned her nursing school debt, the volunteer at a homeless shelter who worked alongside Michael there for years, sworn to secrecy, and the game show host who recalled that after a contestant mentioned she needed £15,000 for IVF treatment, George Michael phoned the show to give her every last pound of that sum, on the condition that the donation remain anonymous.

Before long, word got out that he had donated all the proceeds from his 1991 duet with Elton John, "Don't Let the Sun Go Down on Me," to the Terrence Higgins Trust, an HIV awareness organization, and that his earnings from the 1996 song "Jesus to a Child" were all given to Childline, a counseling service dedicated to helping youth. Publicly, Michael had been one of the biggest celebrities to participate in the famous Band Aid recording of "Do They Know It's Christmas?" and his free concert in the UK for nurses after his mother's death was well known. But most of his other acts of giving, from helping strangers in need to writing huge checks for charitable organizations, were done anonymously. Only after his death did people come forward to acknowledge his generosity.

There is no doubt that in his short life, George Michael experienced his fair share of troubles, but at the end of the day he used the fame and fortune with which he had been blessed to enrich the lives of others, with no expectation of recognition. It would have been easy for him to take a different approach. He could have hoarded his money for himself alone, choosing not to do good for others. He might have doled out elaborate gifts randomly, the way Elvis Presley was known to buy dozens of Cadillacs and give them away like candy as presents for friends and strangers alike. He could have consulted with attorneys and planned his giving to ensure that he got the maximum tax deductions. Instead, he chose to give charity anonymously, not publicizing his generosity, but presumably with the best interests of others as his main motivation.

The act of giving to charity is something we can all agree is good for the world and good for the soul. Helping others is one of the unquestionably positive choices you can make, and opportunities to do so are always just around the corner. Still, while we may carry ideas about giving in the back of our minds, it can be hard to make charity a part of our daily routine.

The choices we make every day, and the actions we take, have long-lasting effects beyond our immediate comprehension. Making the effort to give frequently and consciously—and preferably with anonymity—can impact your personality and the development of your character for the better. As with other aspects of the Secret Life, the act of giving anonymously, without the expectation of getting *anything* in return—even something as simple as recognition—has the greatest long-term advantages for both the giver and the receiver.

We can only guess how George Michael's modesty and his insistence on anonymity impacted his inner life. We now know how much he helped other people achieve their dreams and pursue their careers. But how did his secret charitable giving impact him? I would guess that Michael's secret gifts and donations helped bolster him against the significant difficulties he faced in the limelight, and in turn gave him the confidence and the discipline he needed to focus on his own talent and achieve the greatest accomplishments of his life.

The Middle Path

Meet Julie, an administrative assistant at a dentist's office. Julie works regular hours and makes decent money. She lives in a house in the suburbs with her husband, who also works full time, and their two children. Julie is constantly worried about her finances. Though she is not in debt and her income is enough to provide for her family, the thought of spending on anything "extra" makes her uncomfortable. She shops at thrift stores and grocery outlets, and her kids only get toys for holidays and birthdays. Julie feels a sense of giddy accomplishment when she saves money for a rainy day. The idea of spending on luxuries fills her with dread, and giving money to people outside her own family is out of the question. Julie is what I would call a miser.

Somewhere in the same town lives Sally, a spendthrift. Every dollar she earns burns a hole in her pocket. She loves to shower her husband and children with beautiful gifts and surprise treats, and she doesn't see the purpose of putting off till tomorrow what she can buy today. If she sees a homeless person on the street, she will empty her wallet, regardless of whether or not she will need that money for herself later in the day. She feels she is living her life to the fullest, enjoying every moment without worrying about the future.

Both Julie and Sally act on extreme attitudes that are unhealthy and potentially dangerous. A miser like Julie can quickly become socially isolated, anxious, and depressed. A spendthrift like Sally puts her own well-being at risk by not thinking responsibly about the future or planning for a day when money may no longer be available. Sally chooses to believe that more money will materialize when she needs it, and she prefers to share what she has and live in the moment. Both extremes can lead to problems in family relationships and professional success. Obsessing in any one direction prevents us from seeing the big picture and achieving the level of calm we need to be our best selves.

With charity, as with every other part of the Secret Life, we all fall somewhere along a continuum between the extremes like the ones we see in Julie and Sally. Ideally, we should aim to find a middle ground when we feel ourselves tipping toward one extreme or the other. Maimonides pointed to this Middle Path, the ultimate balance. When it comes to charity, the Middle Path would be donating just enough money that you are neither sitting on a fortune you can't possibly need nor languishing in a state of abject poverty or risking your financial security for the future. Everything, as the saying goes, in moderation.

Not only does finding your Middle Path help you unlock your best relationship to charity, but working toward this balance in one aspect of your life will also naturally lead to greater balance in every other part of your world. Eliminating your tendency to be preoccupied with either end of an extreme frees up your mental and emotional energy so that you can focus on more important things.

Julie's daily life is impacted by her fear of running out of money and her constant efforts to scrimp and save. This means that she is almost always in a state of heightened anxiety. Sally is so consumed with obtaining bigger and better "stuff," and buying gifts for her loved ones, that she can easily find herself without the means to provide for her own basic needs. Both women are unable to achieve the inner calm they need to claim control over their ideal existence. Only by working toward the Middle Path can Julie and Sally neutralize the urges that vie for their attention and open the spaces within to fill with the thoughts and actions that can bring them true fulfillment and happiness.

To reach a balanced state yourself will take some time and effort. Before you can adjust your attitudes toward giving, you should first think about your patterns and tendencies. Are you the kind of person who avoids eye contact with beggars, or one who makes a point of boxing up leftovers at restaurants and actively seeks out a hungry person to whom you can give them? Do you prefer to attend fund-raising events in person or send checks in the mail to your favorite causes? Do you give of your time and your talents as well as your pocketbook?

Once you begin to understand your relationship to charity, look for patterns and think about how they affect you on a deeper level. If you hold onto every dollar you earn, you will soon find yourself unwilling to share yourself with others or to engage in activities that you enjoy. If you empty your wallet every time you come across someone in need, you may eventually find yourself on the begging side of the equation. There has to be balance, and the key to finding that balanced Golden Mean has much to do with secrecy.

How to Cultivate the Secret Act of Charity

You may not be Julie or Sally, with their issues, or Oprah or George Michael, with their bank accounts. But you have a lifetime's worth of experience and talent, and you can always find a little extra cash in your pocket. There is always something you can do, and something you can give, to help enrich the lives of fellow human beings. If you can't afford to donate money right now, it's entirely possible that you can find a few hours a month to volunteer somewhere, or you can organize a donation drive for much-needed food, clothing, or hygiene supplies for the underprivileged.

Above all else, helping someone to find a job or to train for a career—teaching a man to fish, so to speak—is the greatest act of charity one can hope to perform. Even if you don't have a lot of money to share in these efforts, you can usually find some time in your schedule to share your skills with others. Help people apply for jobs or revise their résumés, teach people basic culinary skills so they can find work in restaurants, tutor high school students in your favorite subject, help build shelters with Habitat for Humanity. There is always something you can do to help another person further his or her goals of self-improvement, and in turn you will both contribute to positive global change.

Beyond creating a budget for charitable giving and choosing the causes that mean the most to you, the very best way to become a generous person is by literally practicing the act of giving as often as possible, with scheduled regularity. As with all aspects of the Secret Life, *you can create a desired personality trait by transforming your conduct alone*. Yes, it's truly that simple! Practice, practice, practice! Small actions can lead to profound change if they are done regularly and with the right intentions.

It is far easier to change an action than it is to change an attitude. Consider, for example, how your day would change today if you chose to smile at every person you pass. Every time you walk past someone—friends, family, and total strangers alike—look them in the eye and smile genuinely. You will soon see that not only will you make a difference in the experience of everyone you encounter, but you will feel happier, lighter, and more alive today than you did yesterday. Before long, you will find that your anxieties and worries have drifted further from your mind, and that smiles are coming naturally to you and those around you. If you change your action, you change your attitude.

Maimonides understood this principle. He taught that many acts of giving a modest amount of charity would lead to greater good than a large one-time donation. In today's world, that would translate to giving one dollar a thousand times rather than giving a thousand dollars once. You don't need a lot of money to become a charitable person; you just need an open heart and a willingness to develop a healthy relationship to money and giving. Anyone can do this, regardless of financial circumstance. Even if you can only afford to part with pennies, doing so will lead to greater benefits than you can presently imagine.

Once you've started to give money on a regular basis, maybe by carrying around a separate wallet with small bills so that you will have cash on hand when you encounter someone in need, it will soon become second nature. After some time, you won't miss those extra dollars or cents, and you will begin to look for ways to do more good.

As your charitable actions gradually increase in frequency, they may also change form. You may find yourself looking for causes that are personally meaningful to you and begin to make donations to those organizations in particular. Or you may pick up some volunteer hours at a place where you can use your existing skills to help better the lives of others. This can be something as simple as knitting baby blankets with the residents of a senior center, or weeding at a public park, or donating your unused clothing and household items to Goodwill.

Before long, you will see that repeated acts of kindness and charity will most certainly be transformative for you. Your character will deepen, and you will feel enriched in ways you may not be able to imagine at the start of your journey. The more often you give of your time and money, the less often you will find the need to talk about it with others or tally up your contributions for your own satisfaction. Gradually, you will evolve into a more charitable person all around, and eventually you will even become more charitable with yourself—forgiving yourself for the faults with which you may struggle.

The Secret Benefits of Charity

There have been numerous studies over the last decade that prove how beneficial giving charity is for people of all walks of life. Harvard economist Arthur Brooks wrote in his book *Who Really Cares* that for every $1 you donate, you generate

$4.35 in extra income, $3.75 of which can be directly related to the donation. And this translated even more profoundly to the national level, where for every 1% increase in private donations across the United States, there would be an increase of over $35 billion in actual GDP—a multiplier effect of over 15 times! Brooks notes how many wealthy people are known philanthropists, like Warren Buffet, who intends to leave 99% of his substantial fortune to charity upon his death, and he believes gaining wealth is absolutely linked to giving charity—and results from it. Giving leads to happiness, and happiness leads to success.

Other studies prove that your level of happiness increases when you focus on how the money you donate, or time you spend volunteering, will help another person, and that senior citizens who volunteer in any given year are 40% less likely to die that year than their contemporaries with the same age and health factors. While these proofs are fascinating enough on their own, I have seen how practicing charity within the parameters of the Secret Life can be completely transformative.

For example, if you raise your paddle in an auction for all to see, you may feel a rush of pride and satisfaction that you simply won't find in the private act of writing a check at home for the same amount and putting it in the mail. But how might the secret act of giving benefit you beyond the very moment of making that donation? At the end of the day, if you are the only one who knows what you've done for another person or an organization, you will find that the internal boost you receive is so beneficial and satisfying that its effects can be life-altering.

Being involved in charitable work naturally arouses a sense of *gratitude*. When we busy ourselves with helping others, we begin to truly understand and appreciate all our blessings. Feeling grateful and fortunate then leads to a greater sense of contentment and happiness. And of course, when we are happier and more content, we tend to do more good in the world. This *cycle of positivity* is just one of the many secret benefits of charity.

If your personal goal is to unlock the highest levels of charity and to reap the secret benefits that come with it, you will find that working toward that goal will in turn set off a repeating cycle of blessing and gratitude, pouring positive energy into the universe and bringing about tremendous healing and change. Making any movement in that direction is positive, even if you have to start at the lowest level and work your way up. The very act of trying will bring with it unforeseen benefits.

Beyond increasing our overall *happiness* and *contentment*, doing good for others is one of the best ways to develop your sense of *empathy*. As an essential element of any interpersonal relationship, empathy—the ability to identify with what another person is experiencing—affects everything we do. Having a real sense of what another human being feels is essential to being able to meet that person's most basic needs, whether he or she is your spouse, child, coworker, or the recipient of your charity. When you make an effort to be more empathetic in your charitable acts, that empathy will naturally and effortlessly extend into your other relationships, deepening and strengthening them.

Next, aiming for anonymity in your charitable giving is more advantageous than you may realize. On the surface, you can see how remaining anonymous helps you keep your ego in check and how it helps the recipient of your charity maintain self-respect. But beyond those significant results, giving without recognition helps you develop *self-discipline* at an accelerated pace, because when money is given anonymously, there are no competing goals, like recognition, pride, or honor, to slow things down. As a result, your giving will not be diluted by the accolades you may seek, and you will feel an immediate sense of accomplishment and satisfaction internally. You will want to experience that feeling as often as possible, which will prompt you to repeat these actions time and again.

Regardless of what level of charity you are at right now, working to gain control of your instinctual relationship to money and to uncover your personal Middle Path will lead to a greater balance not only in your personal life, but in your bank account as well. Once you have worked on your healthy emotional detachment from money, you will *be more receptive to business opportunities* when they arise. In other words, if you are willing to part with your money at regular intervals, the idea of investing in a new business venture will be less intimidating. After all, you need to spend money to make money, right? Now that you have released your anxieties about money, you will be more willing to take calculated financial risks and potentially increase your own bankroll. Just as you would wear a business suit for a job interview, hoping to "dress for success," thinking like a philanthropist can often lead to increased wealth.

This is not to say that by giving away money to those less fortunate, you will set yourself up to become a millionaire. There is no magic formula for wealth, and that should not be your goal. Rather, if your intentions are to become a more compassionate person, to bring positive energy into the world, and to transform your daily life into one with increased purpose and meaning, then cultivating your charitable side is an obvious choice. However, a natural by-product of generosity done right just happens to be success.

Every part of the Secret Life is interconnected and contributes to the larger goal of living a more fulfilling life. Practicing regular acts of charity, especially those done anonymously, helps you gain *self-control* and *self-mastery* in every aspect of your life. Training yourself to temper your passions and to moderate your behavior when it comes to money can have far-reaching effects on your day-to-day routines, your relationships with others, and more.

CHAPTER TWO

THE SECRET OF JUSTICE

It is better to acquit a thousand guilty persons than
to put a single innocent one to death.

MAIMONIDES

HE WAS JUST 17 years old, a recent high school graduate. A young black man in the prime of his life, Jarrett Adams found himself the victim of a flawed justice system. He and two friends were wrongly accused of sexual assault by two white women on a college campus, and in a whirlwind of fear and bad advice from a public defender, Adams was convicted and sentenced to 28 years in prison by an all-white jury. That was in 1998. Today, Jarrett Adams is a free man, a lawyer, and a passionate advocate for civil rights and criminal justice reform.

Adams's story is one of justice gone terribly wrong— and then absolutely right. As a young man whose experience with the criminal justice system was limited to watching episodes of *Law and Order* on television, Jarrett naively assumed that because he was innocent, he would be released after a fair trial. Instead, his court-appointed lawyer—randomly assigned to his case because his family could not afford an attorney—suggested he use a "no defense" model, even though there was a witness who could have been called to testify on his behalf. Trusting the lawyer and the system, Adams agreed. It was a terrible idea, and Adams soon found himself facing the prospect of spending the next 28 years behind bars, unable to go to college, get a job, start a family, and enjoy all the other normal experiences of young adulthood.

Jarrett was young and impressionable, and it would have been all too easy for him to sink down into the abyss of hopelessness and rage and engage in the often-violent culture of prison life. Had he given in to those understandable emotions, he might have committed actual crimes in prison, extended his incarceration even further, and irreversibly changed the course of his future. Fortunately for him, he had a cellmate who worked in the prison law library and encouraged him not to give up, but to fight for his life. Adams maintained his innocence and spent the next 10 years quietly studying law books day after day. He studied so much, in fact, that he was able to pinpoint the fatal flaw in his case—ineffective representation by his counsel— and formulate the argument a new lawyer would need to make on his behalf. Eventually, he found that lawyer at the

Innocence Project, a nonprofit organization that specializes in defending the wrongly accused, and his case went back to court. The lawyer was astounded. This young man, who had been in jail for years, had paved the way for his own exoneration. The case went back to court, and Jarrett Adams was freed, after 10 long years in prison.

Once he was finally out, Jarrett did not spend his energy ranting and raging, even though that might have been understandable. Instead, he resolved to make sure he could help others who would find themselves in the same situation. He went to college just one month after being released, and then to law school. He graduated from Loyola University and became a criminal defense attorney. He clerked in the same courtroom where his wrongful conviction had been overturned, and then joined the Innocence Project as a criminal defense attorney. As if this wasn't enough, one of Adams's first victories in court was to overturn the conviction of a man who had served over 25 years in prison for a rape he did not commit, despite an alibi witness who testified that the accused was in a different state at the time of the assault. This man was incarcerated because the jury chose to believe an FBI agent who presented microscopic DNA evidence that has since been proved inconclusive. Not only did he manage to pave the way for his own freedom, but Adams has dedicated his life to helping others who have fallen victim to the same kinds of injustice.

This story is amazing. It proves that the human spirit, given the right circumstances, can be unbreakable. Jarrett Adams is a shining example of making the most out of a horrific situation and persevering to live a noble, purpose-filled life. He managed to survive for years without crumbling under the pressures and conditions of prison life, focusing instead on educating himself and creating a new and improved reality. In essence, during those years, Adams lived the Secret Life, holding tight to his belief in justice and finding a productive way to bear the burden of that challenging time. The persistent, internal journey he took from wrongful imprisonment to emboldened freedom helps us understand what Maimonides meant when he made a once-radical argument that it was better to let a thousand guilty men go free than to convict a single innocent person.

While we all have our own unique ideas about justice and injustice, we can agree that despite the commitment to due process, fair trials, and effective legal counsel, our system too often fails poor and disadvantaged people. And this is America! Consider how unjust things can be in parts of the world where democracy is not established. If we are at the top of the justice ladder and have such an imperfect system, how hard must it be for those who live at the bottom?

Living the Secret Life involves reconsidering our personal relationship to justice. This goes beyond finding ways to make the world a safe, fair place where the "good guys" win and the "bad guys" lose, although this goal is itself worthy and commendable. What we need in order to experience even a fraction of the personal fulfillment that Jarrett Adams has realized is to practice justice in our daily lives, seeking out ways to do the right thing even when that means working against established systems. In order to do that, we must first think about what justice truly means to us, and how pursuing our individual ideals can benefit ourselves and our communities.

What Is Justice?

Charles Dickens wrote, "Charity begins at home, and justice begins next door." In other words, while charity can be a private, personal experience, justice necessarily involves others. So how can it be a part of the Secret Life? Your first random associations with the concept of justice likely involve megaphones, chants, sandwich board signs, or the sharp sound of a judge's gavel hitting a hard, wooden bench. But justice goes beyond the protest rallies and courtrooms of our imagination and extends into our most private relationships. Our parents, children, partners, friends, colleagues, and members of our communities are all affected by the choices we make and the words we use when we express our judgments— something we do daily, often without any true awareness.

We can talk about being kind and fair to ourselves, but the real challenge comes when we are in a relationship. Just as doctors vow to "do no harm" as one of their fundamental priorities, we must always strive to avoid judging others. We judge when we gossip. We judge when we blame. We judge when we look out only for our own self-interest in business, rather than also considering the common good and everyone's bottom line. And when we discipline others, whether as a parent, a supervisor at the office, or an officer of the law, we judge when we do so with anger, revenge, or prejudice in our hearts. How do we contain our instinctive human need to pass judgment on others, for good or bad, or to place our own value systems on others?

Seeking justice is an exercise in consistently looking out for our neighbors, with an eye to the greater good. Just as we would hope to be treated fairly should we find ourselves in trouble, we should always do the same for others. This is not just an ideal concept to carry in the back of your mind and talk about at dinner parties. In order to really embrace justice as a life value, you need to live and breathe it in your Secret Life. In almost every interaction you have, you can choose to give the benefit of the doubt and to reserve judgment until all the facts are clearly and fairly presented, or you can jump to anger and accusation, giving in to instinctual prejudice.

Consider the story we are taught as children about George Washington and the cherry tree. As legend has it, when George Washington was a young boy, he had a toy hatchet that was his most prized possession. Like other boys, he loved to swing and chop things with his sharp little hatchet and did so to his heart's content. But one day, he took aim at his father's favorite seedling, a young cherry tree just starting to blossom. When his father discovered the downed tree, he was furious, and he demanded to know who had done such a terrible thing. Swift punishment was sure to ensue. Little George, full of remorse, broke down and famously sputtered, "I cannot tell a lie!," confessing his transgression. His usually stern father, moved by the boy's honesty and heartfelt emotion, softened, did not punish him, but instead praised the boy for his honest confession, saying that George's act of truth-telling was worth more to him than any tree.

George Washington's tree-chopping incident illustrates an idea that Maimonides presented hundreds of years earlier. Controversially, Maimonides believed that laws and legal systems were in place not only to keep the peace but also to help us evolve in our spiritual awareness. By following laws, he argued, we deepen and enhance our religious and emotional intelligence. Rather than pitting the two concepts against each other, he believed that the rational and the spiritual were meant to coincide and complement each other.

In the case of George Washington, by telling the truth and confessing his wrongdoing, risking punishment, the boy who would grow up to be our first president deepened his own moral compass and learned that being honest and following the rules, even when doing so might bring about personal risk, would work to his advantage. He gained his father's respect and admiration, which in turn helped boost his own levels of self-confidence, a necessary character trait for a leader. As for his father, he learned that delaying judgment and sentencing until the accused had presented his case was the wisest choice, allowing him to appreciate his son's remarkable integrity and strengthen their bond. The ripple effects of this one small act would resonate through-out the course of American history.

Mercy

Justice is completely reliant on the idea of mercy. Not simply forgiveness, mercy is kindness, compassion, and empathy. Maimonides argued that it is not possible to achieve true justice until all the avenues of mercy have been exhausted. This means that we must first and foremost give others the benefit of the doubt in every possible way. Only after this has been done over and over again can punishment be applied justly.

We can also understand mercy as the act of being open-minded and receptive to people in our lives whose ideas are vastly different from our own. In today's society, this concept is entirely relevant. We are living in an age of extreme polarization and political turmoil, and it can be easy to dismiss whole groups of people whose views seem repugnant (and who view us with the same degree of repugnance!), rather than attempting to understand their perspectives and find avenues for productive debate and progress. Just think of how different our reality could be if we took the time and energy to truly listen to others and consider their perspectives without judgment.

When I think of what it means to be merciful, the story that comes to mind is none other than one of my boyhood favorites, Superman. In one classic comic book, "The Death of Superman," the high-flying hero forgives his archenemy Lex Luthor for all his misdeeds, and even goes so far as to build a lab for Luthor, presumably so he can work to invent cures for diseases. Luthor had convinced Superman that he was a changed man, truly reformed. Of course, this didn't end well for our trusting superhero, as Luthor went on to kidnap Superman's friends and force them to watch as he exposed Superman to kryptonite, killing him once and for all.

You may wonder why I bring up this story, in which Superman's generosity of spirit and practice of mercy led to his demise. Good question! I mention it because even though Superman met his end in this story, he set an example for his many admirers about forgiveness and the quest for justice. And once the sad part of the story ends, Supergirl takes over and deals with Lex Luthor, punishing him to the full extent of the law for his treachery. Only once every avenue of mercy had been exhausted was a punishment given. In the end, the bad guy got what he deserved, and the good guys won at long last.

We can apply this story to our own lives, regardless of whether or not we possess superpowers. It may not always be the obvious choice to act mercifully in the face of injustice, and it is certainly not easy to do. Our human instincts are to be reactive, to fight against the "bad guys" at all costs. However, if we agree that every human being has the right to a fair and equitable chance in life, and that we want others to treat us with the same fairness and equity, making that choice gets easier. If Superman can show Lex Luthor mercy, we too can find it in our hearts to treat the "other" in our lives with kindness and empathy.

Sometimes, the most radical thing we can do is to befriend someone. Everyone needs friendship, and often the people who need it most are the least friendly, the most closed off from others. Perhaps there is a cantankerous neighbor in your life. You know, the one who regularly complains online about noisy kids or dog droppings or parties that go past 9 p.m. in the summer. The easiest way to deal with people like this is to quickly appease them and find ways to avoid them in your daily life. But often, those are the people who need a friendly wave or a few minutes of conversation most of all. By going out of your way to be friendly and warm to people who are prickly and abrasive, you show them that they are worthy of kindness and compassion. This simple act of friendship can be truly transformative.

One of the most endearing fictional characters of the last decade is the protagonist of Fredrik Backman's bestselling novel, *A Man Called Ove*. Cranky and antisocial, Ove spends his days complaining about his neighbors and pushing them away in his relentless pursuit of schedules, rules, and regulations. One day a new family moves into his complex, and the family members begin to drive him crazy with their insistence on doing things their own way. Despite his abrasiveness, the family members persist in engaging with Ove and asking for his help. Slowly over the course of the story they get to know the real person below the surface of the grouchy old man.

By befriending Ove, at first against his will, and then asking for his help when they face challenging times, not only do the people in the family gain his friendship and loyalty, but they also transform his life and bring him a new purpose. As the book develops, the reader learns that Ove had been planning to end his life after the devastating loss of his wife. But then this new family arrived, and the family members kept interrupting his suicide mission with all their needs. Gradually, Ove realizes that he has a reason to go on living, because this new young family needs him. The family gives him purpose, and he lives the rest of his life surrounded by companions who care for him. Everyone wins.

Do you have an Ove in your life, someone at home or at the office who irritates you or who always seems to be in your way? Do you tend to ignore or avoid that person, rather than engage in conflict? Instead, consider the opportunity this person presents to the development of your Secret Life. By extending yourself and asking this person for advice or help on a personal or professional matter, you can give him or her an opportunity to be a mentor. Doing so, you shift the balance of your dynamic in his or her favor, which will in turn generate in that person a feeling of warmth toward you, since a mentor naturally roots for the success of the person he or she is advising. The feelings that come with being respected enough to be needed and the satisfaction of having an obvious purpose in another person's life are transformative for both parties. By extending your mercy to someone who usually stands in your way, you uncover the person's natural (but usually hidden) tendency to be helpful, and you correct your own tendency toward being quick to judgment.

The common thread in all of this is what Maimonides might have called "justice in relationships." He taught that people should always be judged favorably, that no grudges should be harbored, and that people should make concerted efforts to support and befriend one another. The lack of this kind of relational mercy—or worse, the reverse of it—accounts for the deep polarization in our society today. By practicing the secret acts of mercy and compassion in our relationships, we can combat these social problems and set in motion a healing energy with global implications.

How to Practice Being Just

We've talked about legal justice and interpersonal justice, but there is also the bridge between the two, which we often think of as "social justice." Pioneers of change like Dr. Martin Luther King, Jr., Gandhi, Mother Teresa, and Malala Yousafzai have literally changed the course of history with their actions, their speeches, and their hard work to overcome the forces of oppression, poverty, and terror. These famous social justice advocates achieved their greatest accomplishments not only because they were well-spoken and brave, but because their efforts were bolstered by unquestionable faith and a deep belief in the causes for which they fought.

"Injustice anywhere is a threat to justice everywhere," wrote Dr. King, perhaps the most famous civil rights advocate of our time. King fought for the African-American community in particular, but he did so from the perspective of the wider world. By healing specific, particular wounds, he argued, we would help to heal our greater society in general. I would suggest that by practicing legal, interpersonal, and social justice on a personal level, we too will inevitably effect change in the wider world, one act at a time.

Everyone wants and deserves justice, but what does it mean to practice being just and living a just life day to day? What are the secret benefits of seeking justice not just for yourself personally but also for your community and for the larger world in which you live? These may seem like lofty goals, but as with the other aspects of the Secret Life, changing one's character to be more just is possible by simply consciously changing one's behaviors and intentionally choosing certain actions over others.

When we try to align our beliefs with our actions, we will find ourselves inclined to be more just and fair in our relationships. For example, if you believe in the concept of honesty (a hard one to argue against), you should strive to be as honest as you can in all aspects of your life. You should make it a habit to express your feelings to friends and family members so that you can improve your relationships. You should point out dishonesty when it occurs and fight against the temptation to be dishonest in your own dealings. If you find that you are occasionally prone to white lies or "sins of omission" when you have the opportunity to come clean and tell the truth, you should make other choices in the future.

Just as you will become a more charitable person by practicing repeated acts of charity, you can become a more just and honest person by choosing to act with kindness and mercy, by consistently performing acts of honesty and integrity, repeatedly, over an extended period of time. If you have a sneaky side, you can get past that by acting the part of an honest person, and gradually you will find that you have overcome those tendencies and become an honest person.

At first, it may be difficult to correct the cashier in a store who's given you too much change, or to return lost property you found and really like. But over time, with intentional repetition, acts of honesty will become second nature. You will know you have succeeded once you no longer feel the fierce internal struggle. It's not that the temptation to act badly is altogether gone, but rather that once the trait is assimilated, you will have the ability and control to overcome the temptation.

When it comes to social justice, the possibilities are endless. Of course, no single person is going to solve every one of the many problems of injustice in the world. But chances are that you have a cause that means something to you personally. Maybe it's education, or women's rights, or another important issue. No matter the cause that you choose, the act of fighting for that cause—bringing awareness of the subject to the public and working to establish fair laws—will necessarily bring about positive change.

Justice is dependent not only on balanced legal systems but also on the commitment of individuals in society to temper their own passions and align themselves with the common good. Evil arises when there is strife between people, and even more so when people consume themselves with greed and selfishness, getting stuck in a repetitive, unproductive cycle of the status quo. When your worldview is broader and aligned with an intention to improve the world and do your best to improve society, you will be less inclined to harm others (and yourself, for that matter) and more likely to seek out justice. Once we are free of hatred, jealousy, anger, and complacency, the barriers between us will naturally collapse and we will find that we can heal our divided society. It's within our power! We can literally change the world, one attitude adjustment at a time, effort by effort.

The Secret Benefits of Justice

Practicing justice in your inner life, being committed to truth-seeking, and reserving judgment, as well as helping to promote worthy causes in the larger world, will lead to many significant benefits in your personal life. You will find that by keeping a level head, practicing moderation and mercy, and keeping your temper in check, you will refrain from making poor choices out of anger. Rather than acting on your intensely personal sense of what is right and what is wrong, aligning your actions with the greater good of the universe will allow you to be more merciful to others and distance yourself from anger.

Some of us are naturally reactive. When someone bumps into us on the street, we may shout at them or curse under our breath. We may use that little misstep as an excuse to be disgruntled and aggravated for the rest of the day. When our children or grandchildren empty a drawer full of neatly folded, clean laundry and use the clothes to build a fort, we snap and worry about all the work it will take to wash, dry, fold, and put away those clothes again. We may, in other words, be used to feeling personally offended by the unintentional mistakes or innocent actions of others, because those actions cause us a degree of frustration or discomfort.

But if we are being honest, when you react impulsively to the guy who accidentally bumped into you this morning or to the child who gives you an impish smile as she doubles your workload, you will soon regret those reactions. Often, you wish you'd taken a moment to center yourself and think about the big picture. Sidewalk guy wasn't out to ruin your day. And your little rascal was just being creative and energetic. They both deserve the benefit of the doubt, and you owe yourself the opportunity to act with kindness and compassion both to the strangers you encounter outside and to the members of your family. Taking that moment to connect with the big picture and gain some perspective helps everyone involved move forward gracefully.

When we give ourselves the gift of approaching these matters with intention and perspective, we will enjoy more benefits than we may at first comprehend. When we refrain from being strict disciplinarians, or from insisting that things be done our way (and only our way!), we improve our friendships and our relationships with family members. Because your attitude affects those around you, your being more open and flexible will mean that you are available for improved interactions at home, in the neighborhood, and at work. And of course, when you extend to others the benefit of the doubt, that same kindness will be shown to you in turn.

One of the books I find most engaging is *The Four Agreements* by Don Miguel Ruiz, who writes that we make assumptions that other people "think the way we think, feel the way we feel, judge the way we judge." Because of those assumptions, we tend to shrink from revealing our true thoughts and feelings to others, afraid that we will be judged negatively and rejected. Contemporary psychologists agree with Ruiz. People tend to conflate their personal opinions with universal reality, which can be dangerous. Rather than saying, "I didn't like that movie; it didn't speak to me person- ally," we tend to say, "That movie was horrendous. No one in their right mind would like it." What we do when we make statements like these is close the door for any other opinion or interpretation. We shut down conversation, express our judgments of others, and make honest dialogue impossible.

By focusing on a larger relationship with the world and the other people with whom we share our society, we cultivate our qualities of self-control, we begin to think before we act and speak, and gradually we become masters of discipline. Of course, we should not practice justice for the sole purpose of perfecting our personalities, nor for the benefits that naturally come with developing our core values. We practice justice to bring greater healing and mercy into our increasingly complex world, but when we do, we experience positive personality development as a natural by-product of our efforts.

CHAPTER THREE

THE SECRET
OF UNCONDITIONAL LOVE

Whatever you do should be done

out of nothing else but pure love.

MAIMONIDES

THE SECRET OF UNCONDITIONAL LOVE

IN 1979, THE Nobel Peace Prize went to Mother Teresa, a woman who was small in stature but great in deeds. Born in Albania in 1910, she became a nun and worked as a teacher in Calcutta's poorest schools for 17 years before hearing her "calling within a calling," to serve the most underserved in the community—the destitute and dying, the diseased and cast-out people of the gutters. She established a hospice, a center for the blind, an old age center, and a leper colony, and all along she worked with individuals who were desperate for any sense of human compassion and kindness.

When you think of unconditional love, the concept of caring for another person with no expectation of getting anything in return, it's hard to find a better example than Mother Teresa. By the time she died in 1997, she had helped thousands of people in the direst of circumstances and paved the way forward for future humanitarians. When Pope Francis canonized her as Saint Teresa of Calcutta in 2016, he said, "Mercy was the salt which gave flavor to her work, it was the light which shone in the darkness of the many who no longer had tears to shed for their poverty and suffering."

The Catholic notion of sainthood involves a transformation. One lives a human life, and then an eternal life of sainthood when one lives a particularly godly life. Other traditions have similar notions of remembering holy figures with titles of respect and admiration—in Judaism the *tzaddik*, in Islam the *wali*, and in Buddhism the *bodhisattva*—and we all, on a personal level, have people in our lives who set tremendous examples and help us teach the next generation about our core values and beliefs.

Beyond the already admirable vow of poverty that she took as a nun, Mother Teresa felt compelled to practice a kind of radical love that most of us cannot comprehend. By caring for people who literally had nothing at all to give back—the dying, the diseased, the completely poverty-stricken—she became a hero to a generation and inspired young idealists worldwide to do more to alleviate suffering in our world. The love she practiced was so transformative, in fact, that it literally changed her from a human mortal into an immortal saint in the eyes of her religion.

Maimonides was one of the first people to articulate the notion of unconditional love. He explained that the practice of any number of good deeds, such as charity and justice, can evolve naturally from simple acts done with the expectation of recognition and self-interest to transformative experiences that are done for their own sake, with repeated actions over time. Like those other aspects of the Secret Life, learning to love fellow human beings without the need to receive anything in return is one of the best ways to develop positivity in our lives and, in turn, to make global change for the good.

One of Mother Teresa's biggest motivations was no doubt her belief in the Divine nature of her work as a representative of her religious order. Because she had already taken vows of chastity and poverty, giving up the physical, worldly pleasures of material belongings and romantic relationships, she was able to focus on others without the trappings of ego and self-interest that plague most of us. Maimonides would argue that even without going to the extremes of joining a nunnery, average people can reach up toward a level of godliness by repeatedly acting out of an altruistic commitment to the Secret Life. By finding ways to treat others with kindness and mercy for no reason other than recognizing it is the right thing to do, we automatically elevate ourselves to a higher consciousness and naturally align ourselves with the higher purpose of the Divine. The trick is figuring out how to get into that mindset in the first place.

The Four Perfections

Love is, or so it is said, one of the simplest and most complex emotions that human beings have to live with. Not only are there countless kinds of love, but within each one of them there are infinite ways in which you can experience the feeling. Is the way you love your spouse exactly the same way that he or she loves you, even if you are both madly in love with each other? Is the love that one person feels for a dear friend a carbon copy of the friend's emotional experience? Of course not!

From the very beginning of time, humans have communicated the beguiling, confusing, overpowering feelings of love. Poetry, fiction, painting, music, and every other imaginable form of art have attempted to articulate the widely variant experiences of love. And yet there is no one description or depiction that can capture a universal experience, because every experience of love is so deeply personal that each one is unique.

The ancient Greeks were especially interested in love. As they approached most other subjects, the Greeks thought of love in terms of science and philosophy and attempted to define the various aspects of it by creating four categories: *storge* (kinship or familial love), *philia* (friendship), *eros* (sexual or romantic love), and *agape* (love of the Divine). Through the centuries, these classifications have remained mostly intact.

When we think of love, we most often think of romantic love, or *eros*, but all four types exist in our lives. And while each type of love is so different from the others, they all have one characteristic in common: they are mercurial.

The intensity of our love for one another and the conditions under which it can flourish fluctuate; this is what can make love so exciting, fulfilling, or heartbreaking. It's filled with dramatic peaks of joy and valleys of anguish. When it's working, it can feel like the only thing worth having. And when it is *not* working, it is all the more painful because it *still* feels like the only thing worth having.

There is only one way to give your love to others so that they don't experience the unstable highs and lows that make love both so sought-after and yet so dramatic and torturous. When we provide a selfless love that has no specific terms or circumstances, even in the face of betrayal or disappointment, we maintain no expectation of any particular outcome. It is given without any attachment to the end result, and with the satisfaction of knowing that giving of yourself in this way makes you a part of everything from your specific human relationships to your relationship with the Divine.

Many people balk at the notion of unconditional love. Some of the best people I know are actually at their worst when in love; they can be petty, jealous, and generally horrible to be around. And just for the record, unconditional love hasn't always exactly been my forte either. I know that the ability to love unconditionally is not an easily picked-up skill set. And what does it really mean, anyway? Should we love regardless of how we are treated? Should we love unconditionally if the object of our affections has no knowledge of our feelings? Should we love and accept family members that have abandoned us when they should be most loyal? Does unconditional love mean sacrificing your own sense of well-being while catering blindly to the needs of others? Ultimately, is there a line that can be drawn that, when crossed, makes unconditional love impossible?

Maimonides taught that there is no such clear-cut line. There's no way that something that's convenient or simple can exist in the world of emotions. Nonetheless, unconditional love does not represent self-sacrifice at all costs in the name of another. Unconditional love is not a form of self-flagellation. It is not a way to martyr ourselves, nor is it a means to create guilt or pressure for someone else to love us back in the way we want to be loved. What uncon-ditional love *does* mean is that we have to love openly. We have to be brave enough to love without guarding ourselves or reserving our full feelings for the other person or Divine entity we wish to foster and develop our relationship with. Unconditional love is the love that focuses on the con-structive, positive creation of a relationship and the whole-hearted cultivation of it.

To truly love unconditionally, and to find or build strong and healthy families, friendships, romantic loves, and a relationship with the Divine, you must accept that things won't always work out as you want them to. You must try to do whatever you can to love unconditionally, giving those you love the best of yourself, sharing yourself honestly, and leading by example.

To get there, as inspired by Maimonides, we can work toward the Four Perfections. These four levels, or stages, of developing relationships correspond to the four basic human capacities, including our capacity to love. At the lowest level, one can share one's possessions. As children, we learn to share our toys with others and take turns. Sharing our "stuff" is the start, but it doesn't require us to give of ourselves. Next comes the ability to be physically involved in a relationship, to literally "show up" for another person, but not necessarily to give emotional support. As we mature, we add a third level of involvement, giving emotional and moral support to our friends and family. And finally, with time and practice, we can reach the highest level, or the Fourth Perfection, in which we identify with others and focus our mind so that we understand and empathize with their struggles, immersing ourselves in helping the other without regard to our own needs. When we reach this level of unconditional love, our joy comes from the joys of those we love, and their sorrows become our own to bear.

As we progress through these Four Perfections, our motivations shift from seeking tangible benefits, to intangible ones, and finally to a state of consciousness that goes beyond benefits altogether. These shifts can be seen in every kind of relationship, from family to romantic to platonic and Divine love, as time passes and practices develop. Our goal, as with other aspects of the Secret Life, is to find ourselves at the highest possible expression of good in our relationships, so that we can bring about the greatest amount of positive change in the world.

Kinship: Love between Parents and Children

There is perhaps no greater love than that of a parent for a child. When we consider unconditional love, it may be this relationship that comes to mind first and foremost. A parent loves a child no matter what, forever, from the instant of the child's birth or adoption. But the truth is that our relationships with our children and, as adults, with our parents, are more often than not fraught with expectations, disappointments, and resentments. We believe that we love our kids unconditionally, but the day-to-day reality of parenting comes with unspoken conditions that we place on ourselves and our children constantly.

We set rules and expectations to teach our children right from wrong and to help guide them into independent adulthood. But the ways in which we express our anger and disappointment when rules are broken or goals are not met often spiral into unhealthy patterns that pull parents and children apart slowly over time. Parents hold their children up to arbitrary standards. Some parents want their children to succeed academically; others give their children so much freedom to create that they neglect to teach them how to function in a society with boundaries and laws. There are parents who try to control every part of their child's life, from who their friends are to what hobbies they can pursue, and eventually, what to study in college and which jobs to take. Often, the need to control comes from a sense of failure in our own lives. We want our kids to have what we didn't, to succeed where we failed. But even with the best of intentions, these conditions place stress on what should be a peaceful bond—the conditions communicate to children that if they fail to meet these expectations, they will disappoint and frustrate their parents, and perhaps even lose their parents' love.

I believe that most parents truly want to love their children unconditionally—such is an ideal to which most people strive. But too often our love is tied to our own standards of behavior and accomplishment. The trick is learning to let go of those ego-driven pressures. If you were a football star in high school, but your teenage son hates team sports and prefers bicycling, either you can push him onto the field and insist he continue the family tradition, or you can take him for weekend bike rides to help him train.

At the end of the day, whether their parents like it or not, children will grow up to be their own people. They will choose their own sports and careers and partners in life. The true, hoped-for influence of parents on children will always come from the strength of the relationship and bond between them. This is what will make the values of parents meaningful to their children and what will make the children want to imitate their parents and perpetuate their values. Parents generally sense that this is all correct in theory, but they realize that in practice it does not always work out. The trick is to work on understanding and embracing this concept, so that we can improve our relationships with family members and encourage those people closest to us to pursue their greatest dreams.

The only way to create those longed-for lasting bonds between parents and children is through unconditional love. When children receive unconditional love, they will know they are cherished by their parents, and in turn these children will cherish their parents. They will then almost automatically pick up on the values and priorities of the parents, without the parents having to say much at all about it. The children will want to make their parents happy, because the children will unconditionally love their parents in turn and will instinctively know what to do to please them. It is in this way that parents acquire true heirs to their own value and belief systems. Ironically, by letting go of our expectations, our children will naturally meet those expectations on their own. Another by-product is that kids who are given unconditional love rather than a suffocating set of conditions are less likely to rebel against their parents—after all, there is nothing to rebel against when you are supported and given the freedom to make your own choices in life.

Of course, a central part of parenting is helping kids understand how to tell right from wrong and how to develop a sound morality. After all, if a parent will not teach a child such things, who will? It's important that children learn to follow a positive, productive path in life. But it's equally important that they know that deviating from such a path will not make their parents love them any less.

When children misbehave, as all children everywhere will do from time to time, parents do best to convey disappointment while simultaneously reminding them that they are constantly loved and that no amount of disappointment can ever diminish that love. Making small shifts in the way you express yourself in these moments can go a long way. For example, instead of saying, "Sammy, you know I love you, *but* I am very upset that you hurt your sister. Go to your room!" you could say, "Sammy, you know I love you, *and* I am very disappointed about the choice you just made. How can we work together to solve this problem?" A tiny shift from *but* to *and* tells Sammy that your love is not dependent on his actions. You both love him *and* feel that he needs to make a different choice and mend the situation. He is not alone, isolated in his room, thinking about what he has done wrong. He is with you, solving his conflicts together with you, feeling loved. When you approach parenting in this way, your children will react positively to you when you least expect it, and you build a level of trust that is unbreakable.

If you are not a parent or if your children are already grown, you can still follow these principles with other children in your life—the children of friends, nieces or nephews, and of course grandchildren. Kids benefit from interacting with many adults in their lives, and adults will absolutely feel a sense of fulfillment when they enter into loving, healthy relationships with children at any stage of life.

Friendship: Platonic Love

Platonic love, the love we feel for others outside of our romantic partners and family members, is one of the broadest categories in the realm of relationships. We can love and be loved by friends, coworkers, and even pets. Animals are some of the best practitioners of unconditional love. Often called "man's best friend," dogs and their humans share a particularly strong bond that can be life-changing. We've all heard stories of dedicated canines who visit the graves of their deceased owners, loyal and still loving beyond the grave, or pets who literally save human lives in emergency situations. But even on a day-to-day basis, the love between a human being and a domestic animal can be extremely strong. Aside from the fact that domestic animals are dependent on their owners for access to food, water, and sanitary care, their attachments are pure and without expectations. Our pets bring us joy, comfort, and companionship every day, and we care for them even though we get nothing concrete in return.

If it is natural and expected to give and receive unconditional love from animals, why can it be so hard to do the same thing with fellow human beings? People also appreciate being valued for the love they give and the personality they present rather than just what they can do for you. Friendships can also be based on genuine fondness, good-will, and shared values, as well as the mutual understanding that each friend will be there for the other come thick or thin, with no expectation of return favors.

In a way, you can think of friendship as a kind of business venture. In business, Maimonides urges each party to a transaction to strive to reach a deal that benefits all of the parties to it and furthers all of their interests, rather than just one's own. Friendship may also be approached in this way, as setting up a win-win scenario. Rather than just focusing on what you can do for me and what I can do for you in return, we can instead give each other the benefit of the doubt and both assume that by giving of our time and energy without needing to give or receive anything in return, we will both come out ahead in life. This is the true meaning of "love your neighbor as yourself."

It may feel frightening to approach friendship wholly "unarmed," as it were. When you no longer look to get some-thing out of a relationship, you may fear a loss of power and self-control. The truth is, unconditional love is the ultimate leveler of the playing field, and that can be terrifying. Our human instincts are to remain in control of ourselves and do what we can to improve our lives. But when we remove the conditions from our relationships, we open ourselves to truly deepening encounters that can develop and refine our personalities in transformative ways.

Romantic Love

When it comes to romantic relationships, the different motivational stages of the Four Perfections are often easy to see. You meet a new person, and all the bells begin to sound at once. There is passion! There are giddy smiles, anxious moments of tension and uncertainty, and intense feelings of physical attraction. At the start of most relationships both partners recall a kind of obsession with each other—you just couldn't get enough of your new partner in those early days. You wanted your partner's face to be the first face you saw in the morning and your partner's voice to be the last one you heard at night. Nothing was as important as this new love—not work, or friendships, or even family. And much of this early stage was about getting the same attention in return, and about the satisfaction that came with knowing you were loved and wanted and appreciated. The desire for romantic attention is so great, in fact, that it often masks gaping holes that pop up later in the relationship.

As time passes and the initial excitement of being together begins to fade, couples start to focus on aspects of their relationship that are less tangible than things such as gifts and physical affection; they begin focusing more on intangibles like how to work together in partnership and how to build mutual respect and sensitivity for each other's needs. At this point, you begin to notice flaws in your partner. It turns out he is not as picture-perfect as you had thought. It seems she has some qualities you would rather do without. And yet you have spent so much time together that it is obviously worthwhile to work through the challenges and find a way to smooth out the wrinkles in your relationship.

Finally, after what sometimes takes many years of marriage and sometimes comes sooner, a couple who have evolved through the various motivational stages of a relationship achieve the final perfection of unconditional love. In a way, this commitment to each other through thick and thin, sickness and health, and so forth, though less glamorous than early love, recaptures some of the intensity of that initial connection. Now more than ever, the two partners cannot imagine living without each other, as their lives are completely intertwined and they have come to depend on each other for whatever comes their way. Understanding that you will care for your partner and be cared for no matter what happens is one of the greatest blessings life has to offer.

Of course, getting to the stage of mutual unconditional love and acceptance is a matter not just of time passing, but of hard, conscious work by both partners. We are used to placing arbitrary benchmarks on each other and to resisting when our partners begin to change or make choices we wish they wouldn't. It takes much courage and dedication to let go of our expectations and the ideas that we formed of each other so early on in our relationships and to let the people we love grow and change over time. When we are able to do so, however, we send our partners the message that we accept them and appreciate them for who they are, and that we do not expect that to change. Naturally, this acceptance is what we want for ourselves as well.

The risk of loving unconditionally is great. It would be easier to let go of a person who disappoints you when your relationship is based on specific conditions—if the conditions are unmet, the relationship ends, and there is a logical explanation. To love unconditionally means that you put yourself in the most vulnerable of positions. You admit that you will love another person come what may, and you open yourself up to hurt and disappointment. But at the same time, you also create a situation in which you can be part of a two-way fabric of ultimate love and support in fashioning your own best-case scenario for the long term.

Love of the Divine

The central prayer of the Jewish people, the ultimate expression of their monotheism, is the *Shema*. Recited twice a day, and again at bedtime, the *Shema* declares, "Hear O Israel, the Lord our God, the Lord is one," and it goes on to quote from Deuteronomy 6:5, "You should love the Lord your God with all your heart, with all your soul, and with all your might." Maimonides understood this to mean that the ideal relationship between humans and God is one of unconditional love—loving not just with your possessions and your energy but also with your very soul, a total devotion to God with every aspect of our own mortal beings.

To love the Divine that cannot be seen or heard or physically experienced in the realm of our daily existence is a true leap of faith—and the ultimate expression of unconditional love. In order to express love for a being that is intangible for us, we can choose to love our fellow humans who were made in God's image, as well as steward the planet that we were all given to live on together. No matter one's religious beliefs, we can all agree that nurturing one another and taking care of our world can be deeply spiritual endeavors.

We can do this by observing the problems between people in our lives and committing ourselves to help resolve conflicts and bring about greater tranquility in the world. Helping other people reach peaceful solutions and improve relationships, without any ulterior motives for your own benefit, is hugely healing and transformative. By acting in a way that reflects our ideal conception of a Divine source—as a harmonious force for good in an often turbulent society—we bring ourselves in touch with that source and improve our own relationship with it. We emulate the Divine when we act out of unconditional love.

Again, we can see a progression through stages in our relationship with the Divine. In childhood we think of God as the giver of all "things." If we pray, we may do so only to request the things we want, and we may try to bargain with God. We say things like, "If I can only get the newest, best toy on my holiday list, I will never bug my sister again. Amen!"

As we mature, we may ask God for more meaningful things, like health and happiness and love, but even then we are not willing to do much in return. It is only when we decide to do good in the world, and to further our understanding of the Divine aim in the world, for its own sake, that we reach the perfection of an unconditional love for God. When we actively partner with the Divine to help foster universal peace and goodwill, we will experience reciprocity in our own feelings of self-worth and satisfaction, even though that was not our motivation for doing so.

You don't need to be Mother Teresa, nursing the sick in the gutters of Calcutta, to reach this level of Divine unconditional love. You can find it by working to mediate conflicts between friends or helping to promote ethical ideals or environmental responsibility. The possibilities are endless!

The Secret Benefits of Unconditional Love

Whether your focus is on familial, platonic, romantic, or Divine love, getting to the ultimate expression of a relationship without conditions takes time and effort. Letting go of expectations, bias, and anxiety is harder than it sounds and sometimes impossible. But once they are removed, negative experiences like stress and depression are often removed along with them, and what is left in their wake are feelings of calm, quiet confidence.

Although unconditional love is not motivated by the character development that results, it just so happens that the practical benefits of the resulting character development are enormous. The character traits you will develop when you commit to loving unconditionally are the most essential, game-changing ones of all. Making the choice to love without conditions requires a great deal of willpower, self-control, and discipline. You will learn to stay calm in the midst of conflict and to approach every situation from a place of kindness and understanding. When you put the well-being of others before your own well-being, you master selflessness and remove the possibility of anger and disappointment. And since only you know that you no longer expect anything in return, the benefits you reap are similarly private, or secret.

What's not a secret is how loving relationships affect our physical health and mental well-being. Scientists have proved that positive relationships—happy marriages, enduring friendships, and the like—lead to a longer life; lower instances of depression, anxiety, and substance abuse; and greater overall satisfaction in life. People who are in healthy relationships heal faster from wounds, spend less time in the hospital, and go to the hospital less often in the first place. This is because having someone who loves you unconditionally, and loving another person in the same way, keeps you in a positive, balanced frame of mind. From there, it is easier to stay on top of healthy habits like exercising, eating well, and going for regular checkups.

We are naturally wired for connection. Having our "village" of close friends, family members, and partners keeps us from feeling isolated and depressed. It's easier to find your way out of a dark place when there is someone by your side to help light the path. And when it's your turn to hold the light and lead the way, you are filled with a great sense of purpose and responsibility that encourages you to take care of yourself as well.

Ironically, through repeated acts of unconditional love, you will naturally develop the qualities most needed to succeed in your Secret Life. Not only will your personal relationships improve, but professionally you will find that you have learned the skills most people spend an entire career hoping to refine—conflict resolution, impartiality, confident decision making, leadership, persistence, devotion, and emotional control, to name a few. What business wouldn't want to hire and promote someone with these skills?

Once we understand that giving love freely is the key to the wholehearted cultivation of the relationships in our lives, it can all start to fall into place naturally. Parents will temper their authority with kindness and compassion, understanding that loving children means letting them develop their own interests and personalities. Friends will let go of conditions and expectations that lead to disappointments and betrayal and focus instead on helping one another achieve important goals. Romantic partners will appreciate each other for their true selves, faults included, and be loved in return. And when we work toward a greater understanding of the Divine will and we align ourselves with universal ideals, we will find that we have connected ourselves unconditionally with the Divine.

Getting there is hard, and the road is filled with traps and bumps along the way, but the difficulty itself has a purpose. When we fail, we learn and grow. When we forgive ourselves for the mistakes we make, and muster the courage to try again, we gain the kind of self-love we need to endure life's toughest challenges. Just as we express mercy in our judgments of others, we can learn to be merciful with ourselves and choose love no matter the consequences.

CHAPTER FOUR

THE SECRET OF A HIGHER CALLING

One finds in himself the cause that moves and urges

him. . . . He cannot restrain himself from interfering

when he sees wrong being done; he cannot bear it.

MAIMONIDES

SOMETIMES I WONDER what my life would have been like if I had been born after the year 2000. Today's young people may have missed out on my generation's idyllic, tech-free childhood sans smartphones and Instagram, but they have the distinct advantage of being born into a world in which information is literally at their fingertips 24 hours a day, 7 days a week. Anything they want to learn more about, they can. Any subject that interests them is instantly accessible. Any person they want to contact is reachable. The possibilities are endless. And as a result of this age of constant contact and immediate access, kids are achieving astonishing things at a rapid pace never before seen in history.

If today's teenagers and young adults are any indication, the future is bright for all of us. What these young people have is an insatiable belief in the possibilities of life. They may be at risk of falling prey to the disadvantages of too much information being too easily available to them before they are mature enough to process it, but for those who have big dreams, that accessibility is golden. For so many of our best and brightest, the age of information is potentially transformative and literally life-changing. Unfettered by notions of what is or isn't realistic, today's youth have boundless energy and curiosity, and they know how to harness that energy unlike any generation before.

Take, for example, The Ocean Cleanup, an organization founded by Dutch inventor Boyan Slat when he was just 18 years old. Slat's vision was to design a mechanism for cleaning the ocean of significant plastic pollutants without creating more pollution in the process. Using computer engineering software and cutting-edge science, Slat designed a passive floating wall that works with the natural currents in the ocean to gather millions of pounds of plastic littering the ocean and funnel them to a recycling collection area. His brilliant idea became a reality over the course of the last few years, and The Ocean Cleanup now employs over 70 engineers, scientists, technology experts, and researchers; has raised over $21 million in donations; and is poised to begin operations. Slat estimates that once the wall is installed, it will clean up 50% of the Great Pacific Garbage Patch in five years' time, saving marine life, improving the quality of the seafood we eat, and bolstering the economy.

Utkarsh Tandon, a high school junior, won a prestigious award for young innovators when he developed a ring that could monitor the symptoms of Parkinson's patients. He then improved the technology so that the ring could also help patients keep track of when they had taken their medications and share that information with their doctors, who could then study the links between symptoms and medications to help improve their treatment. It's a far cry from the model volcanoes my contemporaries built at the science fairs of old!

The list goes on and on, and it extends far beyond the realms of science and technology. John Lee Cronin, a young man with Down syndrome, created a company with his father, called John's Crazy Socks. They sell colorful, fun socks to raise awareness for causes like autism and Down syndrome and to raise money for the Special Olympics. John's company inspires others with disabilities to pursue their dreams and proves every day that anything is possible if you stick with it and work toward your goal. Robby Novak, a young boy with a condition called osteogenesis imperfecta (aka brittle bone syndrome), spreads his message of love and laughter in his popular viral YouTube videos. Novak calls himself "Kid President," dresses in a sharp suit and red necktie, and talks about how to deal with bullying and other difficult experiences with infectious laughter, smiles, and kindness. He chose to take his own personal traumas and transform them into inspirational messages for others. His smile is as engaging as his mission.

Finally, I am awed by the accomplishments of Malala Yousafzai, who was shot by the Taliban at the age of 15 for promoting girls' education in Pakistan, and yet continued to fight for equal rights for women and girls in the Greater Middle East despite death threats, going on to author a best-selling book, to give numerous public speeches, and to become the youngest winner of the Nobel Peace Prize at 17.

When I read about the incredible accomplishments of young people today, I am amazed by how many of them have already been able to pinpoint a definitive mission in life, research how to implement their ideas, and make them a reality. What these kids are doing, seemingly without much trouble at all, is discovering their purpose in life (or at least one of their many noble purposes!). What they have at their fingertips is what some of us might spend a whole lifetime trying to find—a higher calling.

Finding Your Higher Calling

Living the Secret Life is, if nothing else, an exercise in finding deeper meaning in your everyday existence. Changing the way you think about your life from a new perspective of openness to the greater good will lead to significant changes not only in your own daily routine but in the bigger picture as well. All the work you do to shift your consciousness toward making the world a better place has the added benefit of increasing your own sense of personal fulfillment and happiness. What better way to live your new ideas fully than to pursue what Maimonides would call your "perfection"— your ultimate purpose and game-changing goal in life?

Finding deeper meaning in your life is within your grasp if you commit to discovering your higher calling. This may seem abstract or elusive, but it's actually very simple. Just find or get back in touch with the beliefs you value most highly. Think of the legacy you would like to leave behind for your children or for others. Reconnect with what inspires you, and you will know how you can inspire others. Go back in time and remember the things you wanted to do as a child, learning from the pure and unencumbered enthusiasm of your youth. If you spend enough time and energy exploring your own heart, you will find your greatest goal.

The idea of uncovering a "higher calling" may at first seem lofty and daunting. What if you don't have a passion for saving the ocean or the power to stop crime or the intellectual ability to cure cancer? The answer is simple. A higher calling does *not* need to reach global, epic, historic proportions. You can change the world by making a difference to just one other person in this world, or by affecting just one small corner of your neighborhood. If you paint a picture that inspires one person, or write a poem that illuminates one person's imagination, or perform an act of kindness that touches one soul, you will have fulfilled a significant higher calling.

There is no need to make drastic changes or abandon your current lifestyle. Often, the simple act of redirecting the things you already do on a daily basis to advance a noble life goal, and supplementing them as best you can to make advances toward your goal, will be enough. Taking the time to be intentional and reflective, you can accomplish amazing things without altering your day-to-day routine. And doing this as part of the Secret Life, under cover of anonymity, can make the expression of your higher calling all the more life-changing for you.

When I present this idea, I am often surprised by how many people reference their childhood dreams as obstacles to accomplishing this goal. One woman argued, "I wanted to be an astronaut when I was a kid. I spent hours daydreaming about going to outer space. I was sure that my higher calling was to discover a new planet and change the course of science. But I could barely get through high school astronomy. My math skills got worse with every passing year, and eventually I gave up. Instead, I got a degree in English and became a high school teacher. Tell me, how can I fulfill my dream now?"

I understood her frustration. Life doesn't always turn out the way we hope. But she had studied literature. She was a good writer, and she enjoyed her job teaching. I encouraged her to use her skills to promote the work of groundbreaking astronauts, to further space education, to bring speakers from NASA to her local public schools to encourage her own students to pursue their dreams. She could still align herself with the lofty ideals of her youth, and she could use her current skill set to find herself involved on a daily basis with things she loved. Encouraging others to dream and to work toward their own goals may seem to be an indirect path to personal fulfillment, but it has the potential to be extremely rewarding for all involved.

It is possible to recall your childhood dreams and make them relevant to your adult life, even if the expression of those dreams may have to shift to fit into your real life as a grown-up. It is possible to emulate the role models in our lives. It is possible to take the boundless enthusiasm you feel for a subject, or a cause, or a political ideal, and find a way to work that into your current life. There is a saying that the best time to plant a tree was 20 years ago, but the second-best time is right now. There is no time like the present.

One way to ensure that you find your own personal higher calling is to choose a profession that highlights your natural talents or that you are drawn to for reasons beyond financial reward. In other words, whenever possible, choose a "career" rather than a "job," a professional path that leads you along the road to self-discovery. It can be easy to follow the path your parents set out for you, but those paths are often based on their wishes and desires rather than your own. In my own family, it was assumed that I would follow in the footsteps of my two older brothers and become a doctor. I myself wanted to go to medical school as a child. But as I grew into my own, I realized that I was an absolute klutz, and that the simple act of pricking my finger for a blood draw in ninth grade biology filled me with dread. I was not a natural candidate for the healing profession by any stretch of the imagination. Just like the woman who dreamed of being an astronaut but couldn't hack it in astronomy class, I had to find another direction.

Instead of forcing yourself to pursue a career you are clearly not suited for, or doing what you think is expected of you or what seems safe and stable, living the Secret Life will encourage you to choose a career that highlights your natural abilities and interests. If you can find a way to work in a field that excites you and helps you accomplish a deeper mission, you will experience joy every day. For me, that meant going to law school, and working in a field that encouraged the kind of critical thinking I find invigorating, and then studying the works of Maimonides in my free time, teaching his ideas and finding ways to spread the knowledge I found so inspiring and life-changing. Ultimately, writing this book is an expression of my own higher calling, and doing so fills me with an incredible sense of fulfillment and joy.

Although it's not always possible or practical to find a day job that reflects your inner calling and the higher purpose of your life, there is always a way to carve out some time and energy to devote to those subjects in your free time. My favorite example of this is Albert Einstein, the Nobel Prize–winning physicist who didn't do well on his first set of entrance exams to the Swiss Polytechnic Academy and then later found himself working a desk job in a patent office for several years rather than earning the advanced degrees in mathematics and science he so wanted or getting prestigious teaching jobs at universities. Einstein most likely found the tedium of any desk job frustrating, but that frustration encouraged him to finish his "day job" work efficiently so that he could focus on research. And in the years he spent at the patent office, he published several original and transformative papers, including his theory of relativity and the famous equation $E = mc^2$, earning himself worldwide renown, teaching positions—and a Nobel Prize. As Einstein famously said, "Never give up on what you really want to do. The person with big dreams is more powerful than the one with all the facts."

Free Will and Your Higher Calling

How are we to recognize our higher calling if we haven't already hit on it by now? Where is it hiding? Will anything do? By now, you have probably begun to consider the benefits of living the Secret Life and incorporating the ancient wisdom of Maimonides into your daily routines in order to deepen your experiences. Finding and acting upon your higher calling is perhaps the greatest expression of the Secret Life, and the one that comes with the greatest benefits. But many of us are stuck, unable to find the driving force that will push us forward to the next level of conscious living.

Maimonides was a powerful advocate for the notion of free will. In an age in which religious leaders emphasized Divine power and encouraged blind faith, he believed that we have control over our own lives and that virtually anything was possible if one was sufficiently dedicated to accomplishing one's goals. Controversial as these ideas were in his lifetime, Maimonides advised people to take control of their fates and be proactive. If you think your neighborhood, or your country for that matter, is stunting your personal development and growth, he argued, pick up and leave! Find a new place to live. If you find your life limiting or frustrating, stop complaining and start thinking of ways to create a new, improved reality for yourself.

Although these ideas may seem simple and straightforward, they are remarkably difficult to implement, even in our modern times. After all, we are all creatures of habit, and change is hard. Taking charge of our fate and recognizing that we are in fact in control of the course of our own lives can be terrifying, but it is perhaps the most empowering thing we can do for ourselves. Exercising free will and embracing the idea that you are the captain of your own ship will typically lead to a greater sense of happiness and freedom, and it will have far-reaching positive effects for you and those around you. So what are you waiting for? There is no time like the present to find your higher calling and get to work on developing it!

How to Develop Your Higher Calling

Earlier on, we talked about the Maimonidean concept of the Middle Path. By seeking balance in the different areas of your life, such as how you approach charity or justice, you will be able to accomplish great things both internally and out in the world at large. The same thing is true when you think about how to develop your experience of a higher calling. By peeling away the distractions, barriers, and veils of your daily routine and uncovering the deeper meaning you want to express in your life, you can pursue your higher calling while maintaining balance in your life. Rather than creating a big upheaval, just weave it into the life you already lead, repurposing and redefining the intentions of the things you already do in your daily life.

To do this work, you must focus on three important strategies: developing your focus; eliminating physical, mental, and emotional clutter; and committing to stop wasting your time. These concepts may seem basic and straightforward, but they are some of the hardest things in the world to accomplish. Like doing yoga when you are mid-crisis, it can be truly challenging to quiet your mind and ignore the distractions you face and the things around you. In today's world, where we all carry smartphones and technology is literally wearable, and where marketing is targeted to our specific interests on every screen, we are in a state of near-constant distraction and information overload. Trying to disconnect from all of that and let a singular focus emerge takes hard work and a lot of practice. And of course, the best way to accomplish this kind of focus and mental space is by working in secret.

No one else knows what's happening internally. No one else can see the dozens of competing thoughts that run through your head every moment. Only you can truly know which things you need to eliminate from your life and which ones are worth keeping. You can do this work by method- ically evaluating the distractions in your daily life as they occur and making decisions about how to handle them. Do you want to give yourself time limits on how much you will use your phone during the day or how much programming you watch at night? Do you feel you spend too much money on worldly goods? Do you tend to have negative thoughts when positive ones would be just as easy to generate? How can you gather all that information on your own and use it to make changes and better choices?

Without advertising it, you can make subtle shifts in the way you organize your time and the way you choose to relate to the world. This can be done with acts as simple as going through your belongings and getting rid of the things you no longer need, want, or use. A recent book called *The Life-Changing Magic of Tidying Up*, by Japanese author Marie Kondo, became a huge best seller, despite its rather radical notion that if an object does not bring you joy, you should simply throw it away. Kondo gives you step-by-step guidance on how to evaluate everything in your home from clothing to books to mementos, and she draws incredibly strict lines on what to keep (very little) and what to purge (almost everything!) as well as how to keep your few remaining belongings organized in such a way as to maximize feelings of happiness and productivity. The popularity of this book strikes me as interesting, since our society seems so concerned with consumption, while the book advocates minimalism.

What Kondo suggests in her book is very much in line with the Secret Life. Getting rid of clutter in your closets feels great (unless you are a pack rat at heart!) and lightens your mood when you see the new space you have reclaimed by getting rid of things you no longer want. In the same way, casting aside feelings and hang-ups over past hurts that you carry with you emotionally can be equally freeing, if not more so. Your emotional clutter can be as deep and damaging as childhood trauma, or as debilitating as dissatisfaction in your marriage or family life, but no matter what, it can always be dealt with, either with the help of a professional counselor or with time and effort and honesty alone.

There are some easy ways to begin the work of clearing your emotional and mental plate of wasted time and energy without making any obvious, external changes in your life. One is to identify the subjects that preoccupy you and take you away from the time you spend on your ideal pursuits, and to try to limit the amount of time and energy you spend on them. Think about what you truly need to feel fulfilled at a high level and concentrate some of your free time on furthering those worthy goals. Are you too bogged down in your work and responsibilities to make time for the things that fill you with meaning and purpose? If the answer is yes, give yourself a realistic time frame in which to change that reality—for example, commit to spending an hour a week at an activity you find meaningful and love, no matter what. A month later, increase the time to two hours a week. You will soon see that everything else will fall into place, and your work will get done despite the fact that you have added more to your schedule. In fact, you will be more productive and finish tasks sooner with the focus of your chosen path now in the forefront of your mind.

Next is to consider the sources of any negative thoughts and feelings you may harbor on a regular basis—maybe an irritating coworker or a difficult child or a friend of whom you are jealous—and think about who is benefiting from the negativity that those relationships generate. The answer is probably that no one wins. Negativity damages relationships that may already be strained, and it weighs you down and becomes a burden, a veil that separates you from your best self. When negativity next rears its ugly head, try to consciously shift your focus to something positive, to interrupt the flow of damaging energy and replace it with something that inspires and encourages you to express your best self. Rather than fall down the rabbit hole of envy, for example, purposefully make a list of all the things in your life for which you are grateful and joyous. Choose to see what you do have and what you can achieve rather than what you lack and where you have failed.

Once you have made some progress in clearing mental and physical clutter and sharpening your focus to eliminate negative thoughts, you will move quite naturally toward developing your higher calling. Being free to work toward your biggest goals will feel so great that you will continue a positive movement in the right direction, generating more and more positivity along the way. And once that starts happening, you will see the many secret benefits of a higher calling begin to flow in your direction.

The Secret Benefits of a Higher Calling

When we pursue our higher calling along the path of the Secret Life, the benefits are almost unlimited. Because this is such a positive, win-win kind of pursuit at any level, working toward a goal of improving the world, however small, can never be negative. You will find that if you take the time to reframe your daily routine to include steps toward pursuing your higher calling, the benefits will be almost limitless.

In "A Meaningful Life Is a Healthy Life," a scientific paper published in the *Review of General Psychology* in 2018, Stephanie Hooker, Ph.D., M.P.H., and her colleagues explain how having a definitive purpose in your life leads to very real physical and psychological benefits. They note that people who work toward their higher calling have lower levels of stress, better coping strategies, and healthier lifestyles than those who do not have a defined goal. Knowing that you are working toward a meaningful accomplishment means that you don't "sweat the small stuff," that you can put minor annoyances and barriers in perspective and focus on the big picture of what really matters to you. Doing this makes you less likely to worry or focus on the negative, freeing you up for positive thoughts and purposeful actions. When you are less stressed, you are able to think clearly enough to come up with coping mechanisms that help you move forward out of difficult situations. Finally, when you have a higher purpose, you tend to literally move your body more, so that you reach higher levels of physical fitness and health.

Not only does working toward a higher calling improve your own life, but it is also a great way to begin the important work of creating a legacy for your children and their children for generations to come. Creating an opportunity to bond with our kids and give them the example of living a life with deep purpose and meaning, inspiring them to do the same as they grow up, is one of the most influential things we can do as parents. When children watch their parents engage with a subject they find intellectually stimulating, creative, and rewarding, they will know that when they become adults, they will also be able to find their own causes and work toward them. Such goals will not seem lofty or unrealistic because they will have been raised watching their parents doing the same things.

Whether or not you have your own children, having a higher calling will bring about new friendships based on common interests and values, and it will deepen old relationships as well. Working alongside like-minded people toward a common goal that is dear to all of you is one of the best ways to create meaningful relationships that may well last for a lifetime. Finding these new relationships will be so much easier than you can even imagine, because when you are feeling fulfilled by the work of your heart, you give off an energy of confidence and satisfaction that is attractive to others. You become even more interesting than you already were. And the act of devoting yourself to a cause that inspires and fulfills you bestows on you a certain inner peace and tranquility that informs every other aspect of your life. Being a part of something larger than yourself, something deeper than your everyday existence, is undeniably attractive and exciting, and will pull others toward you like a magnet.

Most important of all, living a life defined by achieving a higher purpose is one of our most essential moral obligations in life. Leading an inspired life elevates your soul and brings you to a new level of humanity, raising the tone and elevating your life, immunizing you in a way from the doldrums of life. Oftentimes, people who have succeeded in developing their higher calling describe the sensation as spiritual. It can feel like a higher calling is coming from a higher place, from a realm beyond our human understanding. That feeling of inevitability, as if a Divine source has implanted the idea in our head, can be strange and unnerving, but also inspiring and fulfilling. After all, if a Divine being is guiding us to work toward our goals, those goals feel more important than ever before. Contributing to a worthy cause, and along the way, cultivating relationships associated with this cause, is a kind of partnering with the Divine, making you a vehicle for fulfilling Divine purpose in the world.

CHAPTER FIVE

THE SECRET OF RESILIENCE

When we have a correct knowledge of

our own self . . . we must be content,

and not trouble our mind with seeking

a certain final cause for things that have none.

MAIMONIDES

REMEMBER TED AND Joe, from the early pages of this book? They were the men who looked to be much the same on the subway, but who were in fact extremely different people, approaching their outwardly similar lives in opposite ways. Joe was preoccupied with possessions and wealth and put his relationships and his connections to the deeper parts of life on a lower level while prioritizing professional and financial goals. Ted, meanwhile, enjoyed his success but also used his advantages in life to help others and to set an example for his children of being open and caring for others and giving back to organizations that had helped him in his own time of need. What Ted had over Joe was what we call resilience—an ability to remain positive, optimistic, and balanced despite hardships, and to overcome the challenges those hardships represent in order to grow and flourish. Ted was also a practitioner of the Secret Life, giving of his time and money and dedicating some of his emotional energy to a higher calling, while also working on his primary relationships, so it doesn't seem surprising that he would reach a state of resilience as a result.

Resilience is a concept we hear a lot about today. It is a major goal of modern parenting to encourage children to be resilient—not just to succeed in school or in business, but also to be able to navigate the complexities of our ever-changing and evolving society with grace, compassion, and purpose. Because we live in a time of unprecedented progress and change, we are also subject to a higher degree of social pressure, depression, and anxiety than ever before. Being able to go with the flow and stay positive when things get hard is more important than ever before in history.

Psychologists today are hugely interested in how we can become more resilient, more successful emotionally as human beings. In an age when our culture is rife with criticism, when information—both good and bad—is readily available even when it would be better off hidden away, and when our every mistake as well as success is broadcast for the world to see, it is essential to build up a "thick skin" and learn to take things in stride. Without that ability to move on and let go of negative experiences, it is all too easy to find ourselves depressed or anxious. Worst of all, we have seen an upswing in the number of suicides in our country. In recent years, suicide has accounted for twice as many deaths as homicide, and in people aged 15 to 34, it is the second leading cause of death. With those startling statistics in mind, it is obvious how important it is to build up our resilience.

Ideally, experts say, we should strive to be flexible thinkers, able to easily adapt to shifting parameters and expectations, be optimistic in the face of uncertainty, and regulate our ever-changing emotions. Scientist Leonard Mlodinow's recent best-selling book, *Elastic: Flexible Thinking in a Time of Change*, is all about how we can harness our innate creativity to find new approaches and ideas in a world in which we may be easily overwhelmed by the sheer volume of information and opportunities before us. That this book was so successful is itself a testament to the fact that we are all searching for ways to adapt and succeed when we so often feel like we exist in a whirlwind.

Being able to adapt and bend to new ideas and inventions, and ride the wave of innovation, has far-reaching consequences. Not only will this kind of elastic thinking lead to new inventions and groundbreaking ideas, but it will encourage an emotional revolution that has the potential to change the world forever, perhaps even contributing to a reversal of the distressing tendency in our society toward depression and suicide.

The Secret of Resilience

Fortunately for those of us who have committed to reframing our daily lives within the ideals of the Secret Life, becoming more resilient and encouraging others to do so as well is a natural by-product of all the efforts we make along our journey. By consciously choosing to take repetitive actions that will result in shifts in our mindset from negative to positive, by seeking out deeper meaning for our lives, and by making choices that effect real change in the world, we are creating a resilient framework for ourselves and those around us.

By seeking balance in our lives, we are not deterred by extreme emotions or experiences, and we find ourselves better able to handle challenging circumstances than we would have were we not on our own personal Middle Path. By committing ourselves to seeking out and performing acts of charity, justice, and unconditional love, and by discovering and acting upon our higher calling, we are surrounded by positivity, protected from the negativity and destruction that threaten us along the way. Resilience and inner peace, then, are the ultimate rewards for living the Secret Life.

To be resilient is not only to survive the hardships that life places before us, but to rise above them and to make something positive out of any negative experience we may face. Like Ted, who came out of his brief encounter with homelessness with a renewed sense of gratitude and an appreciation for charity that led him to dedicate himself to helping others in turn, we can become more resilient when we align ourselves with the principles of the Secret Life.

There is a famous saying among Hasidic Jews that goes back many generations to the Kotzker Rebbe: "There is nothing as whole as a broken heart." One can interpret this quote in any number of ways, but what I understand it to mean is that nothing can propel you to greater action than disappointment. Without getting hurt, or experiencing difficulty, you can never fully appreciate the goodness in your life. And along the same lines, nothing is as great a motivator for success as epic failure.

It is easy to be broken by the challenges we face. Losing a loved one, facing poverty, simply feeling that you are not good enough, can be deflating to the point of devastation. The key is to find a way back up out of the mire when life challenges you in the most difficult ways. The good news is that the key to standing back up when life knocks you down is as simple as making a choice to do so. By now, you know that the secret is keeping it secret. By refraining from publicizing every good thing you do and every positive choice you make, you allow the benefits of those actions to change you from the inside out, so that before long you have strengthened your very core and created a protective layer around your soul that will help you bounce back from anything life may throw your way.

How to Find Your Resilience

Adrianne Haslet was a young ballroom dancer who ran in the Boston Marathon on April 15, 2013. When the bombs went off, her life changed forever as her foot and part of her lower leg were severed by the blast. In the painful months that followed her traumatic injury, Haslet struggled with the possibility that her life as she'd known it, her life as a dancer and hiker and adventurer, was over. Facing that sort of physical and psychological trauma might have been the end of her story. But for Haslet, this was just the beginning.

Her story was picked up by Anderson Cooper of CNN, and she became something of a celebrity. When MIT engineer Hugh Herr—himself a double amputee who designed his own prosthetics to allow him to continue mountain climbing after his traumatic accident—heard about her injury, he decided to design a prosthetic limb specifically for her. This bionic leg would allow Haslet not just to walk, but to dance again. Months of painful surgeries, healing, and physical therapy followed, and sooner than anyone could have predicted, Adrianne was dancing again on her new leg. She went on the television show *Dancing with the Stars*, she eventually went back to mountain climbing and other hobbies that brought her joy, and she launched a new career as a motivational speaker and an advocate for amputee rights.

Adrianne's determination to dance again and to not just survive but flourish after her injury is a real-life example of resilience at its finest. On her website, she leads with her life's motto, "I refuse to be called a victim. A victim is defined by what happened in their life. I am a survivor, defined by how I live my life." Adrianne has made the difficult choice to set aside anger and resentment and instead find ways to help others who are suffering and inspire them to move forward and make the best out of their altered lives.

This story is inspiring and encouraging, to be sure, but I feel certain that Haslet's decision to be proactive and positive in the face of devastating change and terrifying experience goes beyond having a good attitude and being lucky enough to have her story broadcast to a large audience. In order to have reached that place, she must have experienced unconditional love and support in her family life, developed a positive attitude toward life and a healthy self-image, and developed her communication and problem-solving skills, allowing her to push through her trying experience and come out with strength and success. In other words, with or without knowing what she was doing, Haslet was living the principles of the Secret Life, and as a result she had a giant reserve of resilience upon which to rely when the biggest challenge of her life occurred.

With any luck, most of us will avoid being affected by such major life-altering trauma. But we can use examples like Adrianne Haslet to help encourage us when lesser challenges come our way. We can find our resilience by choosing to live an intentional life, one with defined purpose and commitment. Repeatedly performing acts of kindness, charity, justice, love, and social action for their own sake, rather than for personal gain of any kind, will in fact pay off in the long run.

There is no need to wait for a thunderbolt of inspiration to hit you. Instead, treat every day as a new opportunity to do good in the world. Keep your focus on your goals and find ways to incorporate those goals into your daily routines. Increase your inner strength and your sense of resilience by the very routines you keep and the choices you make over and over again. Like building up your physical muscles, strengthening your internal core is a matter of practice and repetition. When you choose these practices consistently, you gradually become someone who can withstand more challenges than you realize. And when you are fully committed to the Secret Life, you will not just withstand those challenges, but rise above them and make something bigger out of them.

The Secret Benefits of Resilience

The benefits of becoming more resilient are nearly limitless. Understanding our power to change the world and provide ourselves with much-needed fulfillment and contentment bolsters our self-confidence. Knowing that we have the ability to live in an ideal state of mental and emotional balance, to refocus and elevate every part of our life and fill ourselves with lasting meaning and purpose, we can push through any obstacle that may come our way. As practitioners of the Secret Life, we fulfill our deepest purposes and understand that things we may accomplish are limitless. This understanding has the power both to lift us above a host of trivialities that otherwise could easily drag us down into the debilitating world of depression and anxiety and to keep us moving along a path of positivity and creativity that is unquestionably good.

Through the unique lens of the Secret Life, one begins to feel the sheer wonder of the world and one's ability to change that world for the better. Being aware of your power to make the world a better place is a way of understanding your link to Divine power and to helping fulfill Divine purpose. This realization can be humbling, since most of us are not used to thinking of ourselves beyond the realm of human, temporal existence. But to develop a sense of your larger purpose in the world as an agent of change is one of the most effective ways to widen your consciousness and increase success in the Secret Life.

As you develop your practice of the Secret Life, you will find that you become increasingly detached emotionally from material things like money and possessions and more concerned with the bigger picture of life. Such emotional distance and healthy detachment from these matters allows us to make decisions from a more balanced and rational per-spective in the long run. Just as doctors refrain from treating their own family members because they don't want their emotional attachment to cloud their professional judgment, when we practice the principles of the Secret Life, we hone our focus on the most important things and clear a path for better decision making all around, whether on personal, professional, or financial matters. By constantly, endlessly dedicating ourselves to finding and then living by the principles of our deepest convictions and greatest passions, we prove to ourselves just how strong we really are. With practice, we become unwavering in our positive self-image and our belief that we can in fact do anything. And then we go forth and do those things.

That's the *secret*.

Acknowledgments

THE AUTHOR WISHES to thank Chris Ruddy, dear friend and visionary, for patiently encouraging him to distill Maimonides' most inspirational teachings from his vast body of work, so that many today can be touched by them.

The author also wishes to thank Mary Glenn, who managed every aspect of the publishing process with great care and skill, and with warmth and friendship.

The author is so grateful for the love and devotion of his wonderful family. He also deeply appreciates the many helpful discussions with his good friend Jack Fruchter.

The author would like to acknowledge the classic English translation by M. Friedlander, Ph.D., of Maimonides' *The Guide for the Perplexed* (second edition, 1904) from which certain quotations were drawn.

Finally, the author is indebted to Alys Yablon Wylen for her brilliant research and hard work, support and dedication throughout the entire process.

Recommended Reading

Bokser, Ben Zion. *The Legacy of Maimonides*. New York: Philosophical Library, 1950. Brilliant, brief overview of Maimonides' theology and outlook.

Davidson, Herbert A. *Moses Maimonides*. Oxford and New York: Oxford University Press, 2005. Includes a detailed and thoughtful analysis of each of Maimonides' major works.

Heschel, Abraham Joshua. *Maimonides*, translated by J. Neugroschel. New York: Farrar Straus Giroux, 1983. An informative and easy-to-read popular biography of Maimonides.

Kraemer, Joel L. *Maimonides*. New York: Doubleday, 2008. An excellent scholarly biography of Maimonides.

Maimonides, *Mishneh Torah*, translated, annotated, and edited by Philip Birnbaum. New York: Hebrew Publishing Company, 1989. Outstanding one-volume abridged edition of Maimonides' classic 14-volume codification of Jewish ritual law (with facing English and Hebrew pages).

Maimonides, *The Guide for the Perplexed*, translated by M. Friedlander, 2nd rev. ed., 1904. Classic English translation of Maimonides' major philosophical work.

Weiss, Raymond L., with Charles Butterworth, ed. *Ethical Writings of Maimonides*. New York: Dover, 1975. Contains a nice selection of Maimonides' ethical writings, drawn from his *Mishna* commentary, *Mishneh Torah*, *The Guide for the Perplexed*, and other sources.

About the Authors

Jeffrey Katz is a lifelong student and teacher of rationalist religious philosophy. He became fascinated in his youth by his discovery of the ancient wisdom of Maimonides, and received rabbinic ordination while focusing on disseminating the ancient, life-changing wisdom he had uncovered. He is a practicing attorney, has appeared on national television on a broad range of issues, and has lectured widely.

Alys Yablon Wylen is a freelance book editor and writer. She holds a B.A. from McGill University and an M.A. from Columbia University, both in English Literature. A complete list of her book projects can be found on her website, www.alysyablon.com. Alys lives in Seattle with her husband and two children.

Simple **Heart Test**

FACT:

▸ Nearly half of those who die from heart attacks each year never showed prior symptoms of heart disease.

▸ If you suffer cardiac arrest outside of a hospital, you have just a 7% chance of survival.

Don't be caught off guard. Know your risk now.

TAKE THE TEST NOW …

Renowned cardiologist **Dr. Chauncey Crandall** has partnered with **Newsmaxhealth.com** to create a simple, easy-to-complete, online test that will help you understand your heart attack risk factors. Dr. Crandall is the author of the #1 best-seller *The Simple Heart Cure: The 90-Day Program to Stop and Reverse Heart Disease.*

Take Dr. Crandall's Simple Heart Test — it takes just 2 minutes or less to complete — it could save your life!

Discover your risk now.

- **Where you score on our unique heart disease risk scale**
- **Which of your lifestyle habits really protect your heart**
- **The true role your height and weight play in heart attack risk**
- Little-known conditions that impact heart health
- **Plus much more!**

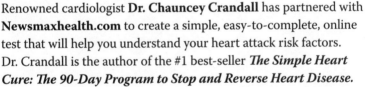

SimpleHeartTest.com/Secret